Own Your Expertise

13 Entrepreneurs Share Inspiring Stories About Success and Lessons Learned in Their Business

©2023

Compiled by Alina Vincent

Own Your Expertise

13 Entrepreneurs Share Inspiring Stories About Success and Lessons Learned in Their Business

© 2023 By Alina Vincent

BusinessSuccessEdge.com

ISBN 978-1-7354408-5-9

Library of Congress Control Number: 2023944193

BONUS GIFTS

This book comes with free gifts, exercises, and resources from each of the contributing authors.

You can access all of them on the bonus Resources Page:

OwnYourExpertiseBook.com/gifts

This book is dedicated to those who strive for greatness and dare to embrace their knowledge, nurture their skills, and fearlessly step into the realm of their true expertise.

Contents

Introduction
Why Owning Your Expertise Is Crucial for Entrepreneurial Success
by Alina Vincent

I remember the day I realized I wanted to start my own business. It was a typical Tuesday morning, and I was sitting at my desk, staring at the computer screen. As I looked around the office, I knew that it was not where I wanted to be for the rest of my life. I wanted more.

In my role as an instructional designer at a university, I loved the people I worked with, the trainings I led, and the challenge of learning new technologies.

But something was missing. I no longer wanted to be held down by the constraints of a job, constantly asking for permission to explore and create. I didn't appreciate that someone had decided what I was getting paid, regardless of how much value I was bringing.

Photography had been a passion of mine since I was a teenager. Whenever I was out with friends, I was always the one capturing candid moments. Over the years, I worked on developing and refining my technical skills and artistic vision.

So, when the idea of starting a photography business popped into my mind, it just made sense. I knew I had the expertise and passion for it.

I took the leap… quit my job and started my business.

Did I know what I was getting myself into? Not a clue.

Did I know what it required to start a business? Not the slightest idea.

Did I know anything about marketing or selling? Not at all.

But it was exciting, and I thought, "How hard can it be?"

And boy, was I in for a surprise.

Starting a business is no easy feat, and I quickly learned that there's much more to it than just being good at what you do. I had to learn everything from scratch—marketing, sales, pricing, you name it. It was overwhelming at times, but I refused to give up.

In less than two years of hard work and a lot of learning and adapting, I grew my photography business to six figures. And it was great.

Until it wasn't.

I made two mistakes with that business that would ultimately lead me down a different path.

The first, I've talked about a lot in the other books in the **Expertise-Based Business Series**: I didn't set it up right. I was trying to do everything myself, which meant I was working 60 and 70-hour weeks. I was exhausted and had no way of leveraging my time or scaling my business.

But there was another mistake I made that I haven't shared yet.

You see, photography wasn't my only passion. I'm also very passionate about teaching. But my photography business was just about creating images and capturing memories, not teaching. I wasn't able to express myself in all of the ways that I needed.

So, along with working long hours and not being able to scale, I was also left feeling somewhat unsatisfied and unfulfilled.

That's when I decided to pivot to a business that involved more teaching. At first, I tried focusing on coaching photography and visual branding, but it still didn't feel quite right.

So, I pivoted again, and this time, I found my profitable niche—coaching and helping others build their own online businesses.

Everything finally fell into place. I now had a business that was based on my expertise, aligned with my passions, and met a need in the market. It grew to over a million dollars in just the first four years.

This book, *Own Your Expertise*, is all about finding YOUR winning idea at the intersection of your passion, expertise, and monetization opportunities. It's a guide for anyone who wants to turn their knowledge and skills into a profitable business doing what they love.

The Expertise-Based Business Series is a collection of books that dives into different aspects of building a profitable business around your expertise, each with its own focus.

The first book, *Teach Your Expertise*, explains how you can create educational content and online programs by sharing your existing knowledge and experience. It's a practical guide for turning your expertise into digital products that can be sold online.

The second book, *Leverage Your Expertise*, shows you how to use online programs to create scalable and leveraged business that can free up your time and grow your business while working less.

The third book, *Monetize Your Expertise*, focuses on addressing the mindset and money blocks that might prevent you from creating a profitable business and covers specific step-by-step strategies to price, package, and monetize your offers.

To be honest, the book you are holding in your hands right now, *Own Your Expertise*, should have been the first in this series. That's because discovering, claiming, and owning your expertise is where it all begins. It's the foundation for creating a business that aligns with your passions and your values… one that can lead to both personal and financial success.

You might have picked this book because you are just starting to think of creating a business and not sure how to identify your most marketable expertise.

Or maybe you have an existing business, and you know you are amazing at what you do, but you can't find an easy way to express your expertise and the value of what you do.

Or maybe you are reading this because you are multi-talented and multi-passionate, and you can't choose which expertise, skills, and talents you should be building your business around, and you know it's holding you back.

Either way, you've come to the right place!

In this book, we'll explore the importance of owning

your expertise, the obstacles that can prevent you from doing so, and practical steps you can take to embrace and communicate your unique value proposition to the world.

Not only will it offer you insights and guidance to help you claim your expertise with confidence, but you'll also find real stories of entrepreneurs who have overcome similar challenges and embraced their expertise.

When you fully claim your experience and pinpoint your profitable niche, you'll have:

- **Improved brand recognition and awareness:** As you become known for your expertise, people will start associating your brand with that particular area of knowledge or skill. This can help improve brand recognition and awareness, making it easier for potential clients or customers to find you.

- **The ability to command higher rates for your services or products:** As an expert, you bring a unique set of skills and experience to the table that others may not have. This allows you to charge higher rates for your services or products than someone without that level of expertise.

- **More opportunities to collaborate with other experts in your field:** Owning your expertise can open doors to collaborations with other experts in your industry. Collaborating with others who share similar knowledge and skills can lead to new ideas, valuable connections, and increased exposure for both parties.

- **More effective marketing messaging to attract ideal clients or customers:** When you own your expertise, it becomes much easier to market yourself and your business. You know what sets you apart from others in your field and can use that knowledge to create targeted messaging that resonates with potential clients or customers.

- **Influence and authority in your field, which in turn greatly increases your visibility and reach**: Owning your expertise means you have a deep understanding of the ins and outs of your industry. This knowledge allows you to speak with confidence, share valuable insights, and establish yourself as a thought leader in your field. As a result, people will be more likely to seek out your advice or services, which can greatly increase your visibility and reach.

- **More referral opportunities:** When you own your expertise, people are more likely to refer others to you because they see you as the go-to expert in your field. This makes it easier for you to generate new business through referrals without having to actively seek out new clients.

- **Opportunities to share knowledge through speaking engagements, webinars, or writing articles or books:** Owning one's expertise opens up opportunities to get invited to speak at events, which further enhances your reputation within your industry; similarly, writing articles/books helps you further position yourself as an expert on your topic.

- **Increased confidence in networking and public speaking situations:** Speaking about topics within one's area of expertise comes naturally, which leads to greater confidence when it comes time for public speaking engagements or networking events.

- **Client attraction:** When people perceive you as an expert in your field, you don't have to chase clients. They are more likely to seek out your services rather than the other way around. By owning one's expertise, business owners don't have to spend time chasing down leads or trying to convince people of their value proposition; instead, they can focus on delivering exceptional service while building long-term relationships with clients who appreciate their unique skills and abilities.

Discovering my own sweet spot for my business was a life-changing experience. Not only did it allow me to provide for my family financially, but it also gave me the opportunity to impact thousands of entrepreneurs around the world.

Thanks to this success, my husband and I were able to travel the world with our kids and extended family. We finally achieved the time and money freedom so many people seek when they start their own businesses.

But what's truly fulfilling is sharing my expertise and seeing the transformation it creates in others. It's the driving force that motivates me every day.

With the right mindset, skills, and guidance, you too can turn your expertise into a thriving business that brings both financial freedom and personal fulfillment.

The beginning of any entrepreneurial journey starts with the awareness that you possess something special and unique.

Yet many aspiring business owners have a hard time recognizing and expressing their expertise.

The Merriam-Webster dictionary defines an expert as "someone with the special skill or knowledge representing mastery of a particular subject, derived from training or experience."

In other words, being an expert means you know more than most in a certain area.

The surprising struggle many business owners go through when looking at their expertise is that they often underestimate the knowledge, skills, and experience they already have in their specific field. They also routinely overestimate how much everyone else around them (including their potential clients) actually knows and understands their topic.

No wonder so many entrepreneurs believe they need to be working in their business for years before they can claim their expert status. This is also how many get stuck choosing the right focus for their business.

The good news is that you are already an expert in something! I guarantee it! You already have something inside you that others need, even if you haven't recognized or embraced it yet.

Your expertise could come from:

- Education (formal degrees, online programs, certifications, or trainings)

- Research

- Practice

- Real-life experience

- Past careers, business, and work experience

- Divine downloads

- Natural talents and abilities

Most people have a combination of these sources contributing to their expertise.

One of the keys to owning your expertise is realizing that you are enough, precisely as you are at this moment!

You don't need another degree or training.

You don't need another certification.

You don't need someone's approval or permission.

You don't need 10 more years of experience.

You already possess a unique blend of valuable assets that can be used to build a thriving business: skills, gifts, talents, insights, expertise, knowledge, and accumulated experiences.

This book acts as a guide to uncovering and pinpointing your most valuable expertise.

Every moment in your life has led you to this point. Every challenge, triumph, setback, and lesson has played a pivotal role in shaping your journey, providing invaluable wisdom on how to forge ahead, overcome obstacles, reinvent yourself, or expand upon your success.

As an individual, you have navigated a unique path that no one else has traveled, making you the only one in the world with your specific combination of background, experience, knowledge, and expertise.

There are people all over the globe who need exactly what you know… what you have learned and faced. They need information only you can provide, explained in a way only you can deliver.

And that's exactly why you should never compare yourself to other experts. No two experts are alike because no two life journeys are alike.

Once you fully understand and embrace this, you will begin to look at your entire life as a source for discovering and sharing your expertise. You'll be unstoppable.

So, are you ready to be seen as an expert?

The truth is, if you want to own your expertise, you must take these three pivotal steps:

STEP 1: Embrace visibility.

You need to be visible, stop hiding, and boldly share your message with the world! You cannot wait for people to discover your talents; instead, you must shine the light on them for the world to see.

It also means that you have to start owning your expertise by talking about yourself as an expert and acting like one even if you don't quite feel confident yet.

If it feels uncomfortable, try shifting your thinking from self-doubt (*Am I good enough? Do I have enough experience?*) to focusing on people you want to serve and whose lives you could transform.

STEP 2: Choose ONE area of expertise to highlight.

Choosing one area of expertise is often the most daunting step, stopping even the most talented, creative, and brilliant entrepreneurs from being recognized as experts.

If you attempt to help *everyone* with *everything*, you'll never emerge as the go-to expert in any field. The broader your offers and messages, the more diluted and confusing your message becomes. To truly own your expertise and create a profitable business, you must identify your most marketable knowledge or skill and focus on it.

STEP 3: Commit to ONE area of expertise for at least a year.

By committing to one area of expertise for a year (especially if you're just starting out), you will establish a solid reputation, trust, and loyalty in your field.

This level of focus allows others to recognize your specific expertise and gives them time to understand what you can do for them and the value you provide. In addition, focusing on one area allows you to perfect your marketing message, gain a deeper understanding of your ideal audience, and increase confidence in your abilities.

It really can be that simple.

Exercise 1: What's Been Holding You Back?

(Download the companion workbook with all exercises here: OwnYourExpertiseBook.com/gifts.)

I invite you to take a moment to pause and reflect on your journey. Ask yourself, "What's been holding me back from fully owning my expertise?"

Grab a piece of paper and start writing down your thoughts.

Is it fear that's been holding you back? If so, what's underneath that fear?

Are you struggling with feelings of being an imposter and afraid of being exposed as a fraud?

Perhaps you're afraid that by narrowing your focus to one area of expertise, you'll lose clients or be "pigeonholed."

Or are you unsure of which area of your expertise is the most marketable?

Are you afraid of making mistakes or failing? Or is it a fear of success?

Or maybe you're uncomfortable with being visible and known?

Are you uncertain about how to differentiate yourself and your services from others in your industry?

Are you constantly comparing yourself to others?

Or is it something else?

Whatever it may be, take the time to dig deep and be honest with yourself. Reflecting on these questions can spark clarity and help you overcome the obstacles preventing you from owning your expertise.

With this awareness, it will be easier for you to take the necessary steps to start claiming your expertise and creating a business around it.

And now, I invite you to make a decision to fully step into your power and embrace the amazing expert I know you are. Even if you are not yet fully clear on what expertise you should focus on (we will cover it in the next chapter), you have what it takes… I promise!

Claiming your expertise is a decision.

Owning your expertise is a decision.

Telling the world about your expertise is a decision.

Are you ready to make it?

If you are, stand up right now. Relax your shoulders. Lift your head. Say out loud, "***I'm an expert, and I'm ready to own my expertise."***

Next, I challenge you to make a public declaration of your commitment to claim and embrace your expertise. Whether it's creating a social media post, doing a live broadcast, telling your friends, sending out an email, or shouting from the rooftops, make your voice heard!

In the next two chapters, I'm going to walk you through a series of exercises designed to help you understand the value of your unique expertise and experience, connect it with your passion, and ensure you are creating a solution that your ideal clients will invest in.

My hope for you is that you'll be inspired and informed… that you'll believe *your dream is possible.*

This book is filled with practical strategies and methods to help you own your expertise and build a business that makes a big impact and ultimately hits that six- or seven-figure mark.

Along with sharing the exact strategies I used in my business, 12 of my clients share their journeys of discovering and owning their expertise, too.

I, along with all of the entrepreneurs featured in this book, want you to learn from our stories, mistakes, and lessons learned, so you can take the right actions and fast-track your success.

And, as a BONUS, we're also supporting you with a multitude of free gifts to uplevel your life and business based on our own unique expertise.

You'll find them all on the Resource Page, here:

OwnYourExpertiseBook.com/gifts

Chapter 1
At the Intersection of Passion and Expertise
by Alina Vincent

Expertise Inventory

Owning your expertise starts by recognizing and claiming skills and knowledge you already possess, identifying what sets you apart from everyone else, and then leveraging it to build a business that will help others.

In this chapter, we'll walk through the process of creating an inventory of your existing talents, skills, experiences, and expertise.

Exercise 2: Professional Expertise Inventory

Let's begin by grabbing a sheet of paper to write down your answers to the Professional Expertise Inventory questions.

While it is of course possible to type out your responses on a computer, did you know that putting pen to paper activates areas of the brain that typing doesn't? Not only does writing by hand help you focus more on your thoughts, but it also connects your thoughts with feelings and emotions. So, I highly recommend that you use paper for all of the exercises in this book, including this one. This way, you can maximize the benefits of introspection and elevate your self-discovery journey to own your expertise.

As you complete this exercise, write down the first thing that comes to mind without editing yourself. Don't hold back or overthink your answers.

And remember, what makes your expertise unique and valuable is the *path* that brought you here and everything you've learned and discovered along the way. Make sure that you are not only focusing on things you are currently doing; you want to review your entire life.

Here are the 30 Professional Expertise Inventory Questions:

1. What business or professional areas do you have years of experience in?

2. Which industries do you have a high level of understanding or knowledge in?

3. What topics have you researched extensively, studied, or read about?

4. What special education, training, courses, programs, qualifications, or certifications have you received?

5. What past jobs, positions, careers, "side gigs," and business experiences have you had?

6. In which areas do you have special "insider" knowledge?

7. In which areas have you received special recognition or awards?

8. What are some innovative or creative solutions you've come up with to solve a problem?

9. What challenges have you overcome in your professional life or in running a business? How did you do it?

10. In which areas do you consider yourself more knowledgeable than an average person?

11. List the topics of books, articles, or blogs you've written or would like to write.

12. List podcasts, YouTube channels, and radio or TV shows you've created or would like to create.

13. What systems, processes, or programs have you created?

14. What have you taught others?

15. What do people come to you for help with?

16. What expertise or services have people paid you for?

17. What are you currently known for?

18. What were you known for in the past?

19. What are you really good at?

20. What comes easy to you? What comes naturally?

21. What topics can you talk or write about for hours?

22. What did you fail at before that you now excel at?

23. What do others compliment you on and ask questions about?

24. If your past clients, friends, or family had to describe your expertise in one sentence, what would they say?

25. What significant life events or experiences made an impact on who you are today?

26. What unique talents, gifts, abilities, and skills do you have?

27. What skills have been the most useful in different roles throughout various stages of your life?

28. What sets you apart from others in your field?

29. What are some unique perspectives or unconventional approaches you bring to all you do?

30. In which areas do you consider yourself an expert?

At this point, you should have a pretty good list of skills, knowledge, and expertise you've acquired throughout your life journey.

How does it feel?

Have you made any major discoveries?

Are you starting to see any patterns emerge?

Next, I would like to invite you to complete another exercise to help you recognize and acknowledge your life experiences.

Exercise 3: Life Expertise Inventory

We're going to look beyond your professional skills now and consider *everything* you've been through in your life. This will be especially helpful if you still don't think you have enough professional knowledge and expertise to consider yourself an expert.

Our lives are incredibly intricate and complex, and we learn new life lessons pretty much every day. Every single experience you have ever had has played a role in shaping who you are today and has given you a unique perspective that you can share with the world.

So, guess what?!

You are already an expert in your life, and I have no doubt that you have some incredible insights and expertise others need. Don't discount this expertise as something less valuable than the skills you learn on a job.

The goal of this **Life Expertise Inventory** exercise is to start recognizing and acknowledging all the different aspects of your unique journey.

It might also help you flesh out areas of your unconscious competence. These are skills and knowledge you possess without even realizing it, often acquired through repeated practice or pursuing something you love. When you practice a task so much that it becomes second nature, or when you are born with a natural talent, you may not recognize it as a unique expertise. When something comes effortlessly to us, we usually don't view it as special or valuable.

However, this type of expertise can be incredibly valuable to others who lack the knowledge or skills necessary to perform a task or solve a particular problem. For instance, someone who's enthusiastic about gardening might not realize that their knowledge in this area is a form of expertise that others could benefit from.

So, let's do this.

Take out a fresh sheet of paper and write down your answers without censoring yourself. Let your thoughts flow freely to truly capture everything that makes you who you are.

There are five major areas of life you'll want to look at:

1. Money

2. Relationships (from romantic relationships to relationships with your children, parents, family, friends, or colleagues)

3. Health and Wellness

4. Spirituality

5. Special Interests (hobbies, interests, passion projects, or extracurricular activities)

For each of these areas, ask yourself:

- What is your story related to this area of your life?

- What have you experienced?

- What have you struggled with?

- What have you overcome?

- What came easy to you?

- What do you know now that you wish you knew before?

- What have you mastered?

- What are your beliefs, insights, and philosophies in this area of your life?

- How can you improve other people's lives based on what you know and experienced?

- Do others notice and acknowledge your transformation, accomplishments, and success in this area?

- Who have you helped in this area of their life and

how?

Let's take a look at the area of money. Here are some sample questions you can explore around the topics of money, wealth, and finances:

- What is your "money story"?

- Do you consider yourself wealthy? Has it always been this way?

- Do you have an abundance mindset? Has it always been this way?

- How have you grown in terms of money management?

- Have you ever managed other people's finances?

- Do you have a good system for budgeting, saving, or spending money?

- How do you feel about earning money?

- How do you view financial success?

- How do you handle financial setbacks?

- How do you feel about asking people for money or selling your products or services?

- Are you good at sales conversations?

- What is your relationship with debt?

- Have you been through bankruptcy?

- Have you inherited or won a lot of money?

- Has money ruined relationships for you?

- Have you been the sole breadwinner?

- Are you financially ready for retirement?

- Are you good at investing money?

- Do you have conversations about money with your partner? With your children?

- Who manages the finances in your household?

- What money beliefs did you grow up with? How did they affect you?

- What beliefs and money blocks have you had to overcome?

- What finance skills came naturally to you, and which ones have you had to develop over the years?

- List significant transformation moments and events that define your relationship with money today.

- What lessons about wealth and money have you learned over the years?

- What are your biggest wins and success stories around money?

- Do people come to you for advice around money?

- What special advice or expertise can you share with people who want to avoid what you've been through or create what you have?

Take your time. When you're finished, go through this exercise again for each of the other four areas: relationships, health and wellness, spirituality, and special interests.

Once you are done with both the Professional Expertise Inventory and the Life Expertise Inventory exercises, take a look at them side by side and identify some common threads between your answers.

Do your professional and personal expertise overlap?

What stands out the most?

What connections can you make between the different skills and knowledge you've acquired?

How can your expertise be used to help others?

Take a few moments to reflect on this, and then **select up to five top areas of expertise** that you'd like to claim and own.

I hope by now you see that your life journey has given you unique expertise that has the power to inspire and benefit others. It's time for you to realize and acknowledge the significance of what you have to offer and share it with the world!

Next, we'll explore how to refine your expertise further and identify the most marketable one to build your business upon.

Tap into Your Passion

You might think that right now would be a good time to start talking about narrowing down your niche and focusing on just one area of expertise. Right?

After all, I did say earlier that choosing ONE area of expertise is the key to building a profitable business.

But… not so fast.

Creating a successful expertise-based business goes beyond simply sharing your unique knowledge and expertise.

It also means understanding your WHY for choosing this topic—why sharing this specific expertise excites you, lights you up, and is central to who you are.

When you combine your expertise with your passion, it creates the ultimate recipe for success.

Expertise represents your acquired knowledge and experience in a particular field, while passion represents the excitement and enjoyment you derive from it.

Your passion is the energy, drive, enthusiasm, and sheer love for what you do that originates from your heart.

Building a business around something that you are good at but lack passion for won't take you very far. If you can do something really well, but it doesn't fulfill you on a soul level, you most likely won't stick to it for very long. Pretty soon, it will feel like a chore or a job.

On the other hand, if you are passionate about what you do, you will recover from setbacks more quickly and have the motivation to keep going even during challenging times. You're also more likely to continue learning and growing.

Success demands a great deal of energy, and nothing fuels your spirit like the internal passion you feel for your topic or the solutions you offer. Passion is a spark that ignites creativity, inspires new ideas, and breathes life into everything you do.

However, passion alone cannot guarantee success.

The familiar advice to "follow your passion" may be misleading. Truth is, you need more than passion to start a business.

You could be bursting with enthusiasm for a topic, but if you lack the skills and expertise to serve your clients, your business is bound to fail. Most people who start a business driven solely by passion struggle with focus and lack a plan for monetizing their passion and creating value for their clients.

Without a solid foundation of knowledge or experience, relying solely on passion will make it nearly impossible to succeed.

So, let's explore your passions.

Exercise 4: Find Your Passion

Below, you'll find a list of 30 thought-provoking questions designed to help you discover what drives you.

Answer as many of these as you can, and write down your responses on a new sheet of paper. Once again, let your mind freely flow, and don't censor yourself. Write down every little detail that comes up, even if it may seem irrele-vant to your business.

1. What are you passionate about?

2. What motivates or excites you the most?

3. What are your interests or hobbies?

4. What are your values?

5. What lights you up?

6. What fascinates you?

7. What or who inspires you?

8. What makes you feel most alive?

9. What feeds your soul?

10. What is your calling?

11. What do you believe in?

12. What gives your life meaning?

13. What activities make you lose track of time?

14. What makes you feel in the flow?

15. What do you love to create or make?

16. What topics do you love to learn or read about?

17. What topics or issues do you have a lot of opinions about?

18. What gives you a sense of purpose in your life?

19. What did you enjoy doing as a child?

20. What is something you absolutely love doing?

21. What gets you to jump out of bed in the morning, excited to start the day?

22. What makes you feel enthusiastic or excited?

23. What kind of work do you do that you find most rewarding?

24. What gives you a sense of accomplishment?

25. What gives you a sense of deep satisfaction and fulfillment?

26. If money was not a factor, what would you spend your time doing?

27. Are you on a mission to create a change in the world or start a movement?

28. What kind of legacy do you want to leave behind?

29. What's your reason for doing what you do?

30. What's your purpose?

Once you are done, review everything you just wrote down.

Are you seeing patterns and trends? Are you seeing your top passions emerging?

Your next task is to narrow it down to five (or less) of your top passions. Yes, even if you identify yourself as multi-passionate, please narrow it down to the top five.

Exercise 5: Find Your Sweet Spot

Now, let's explore where your expertise and passions intersect and overlap.

Grab a fresh sheet of paper and divide it into two columns.

In the first column, list the top areas of expertise you've identified in the Expertise Inventory Exercises two and three. Feel free to include up to five of them.

In the second column, list your top passions from the Find Your Passion Exercise (up to five passions).

Now, take a moment to review both columns and identify the areas where your passions and expertise align the most.

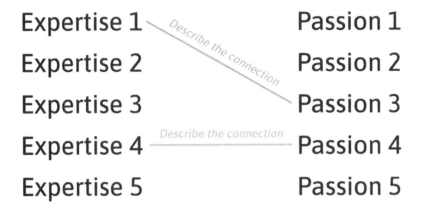

Expertise 1 — Describe the connection — Passion 1

Expertise 2 — Passion 2

Expertise 3 — Passion 3

Expertise 4 — Describe the connection — Passion 4

Expertise 5 — Passion 5

Once you've found these pairs, draw a line between the elements and describe how they're connected. For instance, you might ask yourself how your passion supports your expertise, or how the two concepts relate to each other.

Keep in mind that you can have multiple connections between the elements on your sheet. Each of your passions could support multiple areas of expertise, and vice versa.

Getting Clients Online — Teaching — Simplifying

In fact, the more interests and passions connect with a specific expertise, the better. It's often a sign that you are on the right path, and you'll feel more fulfilled if you end up choosing that area of expertise.

To help you understand this process, let's look at an example:

One of my areas of expertise is helping entrepreneurs get clients online.

One of my passions is teaching. I also enjoy simplifying complex concepts, ideas, and processes into easy-to-follow actionable steps.

In this scenario, both of my passions complement and relate to my expertise, because I use them when teaching business owners how to get clients online using my step-by-step formulas.

It's possible that you may not see a connection between one of your chosen areas of expertise and your passions. That's perfectly fine and actually beneficial, because it provides clarity on what you should focus on moving forward.

Your task now is to identify up to three connections that have the strongest overlap and alignment between your areas of expertise and passions. By doing so, you're taking a significant step toward narrowing down your niche and focusing on one area of expertise that truly resonates with you.

However, we're not quite there yet.

In order for you to actually have a business versus a hobby, you need to make sure your expertise is profitable. In other words, you want to ensure that there's a demand for what you offer.

Having passion and expertise in a particular area is undoubtedly an excellent starting point for building a successful business, but without validating the need for your product or service, you risk investing valuable time and resources into something that may not generate revenue.

Determining if there's a viable market for what you offer also helps you tailor your messaging, refine your offerings, and hone in on your ideal customer. And that's exactly what we are going to explore in the next chapter.

If you haven't already, don't forget to grab the companion workbook that contains all of the exercises from these chapters, along with all of the other contributors' gifts, here:

OwnYourExpertiseBook.com/gifts

Chapter 2
The Key to Making Your Expertise-Based Business Profitable
by Alina Vincent

Profitable Market

In the exercises and explorations we've done so far, we've focused on self-discovery—what we know, what we love, what we are passionate about, and what we want to share with others.

Can you see that it's somewhat one-sided?

So, what's the missing element to creating a truly successful and profitable business?

If you guessed "the right audience that is hungry for what you have to offer," you are right!

The last key ingredient is the profitable market.

Once you've aligned your passion and unique expertise in your business, it's crucial to ensure that there is a demand for your offer.

Otherwise, you may end up like many entrepreneurs who love what they do, but struggle to make sales. This is not the outcome you want, right?

And that's why, in this section, we're focusing on pinpointing your most marketable expertise, so you can not only love what you do, but also get paid for it. This is where the concept of finding a niche comes in.

Your expertise refers to your skills, talents, gifts, strengths, knowledge, and experience, while your passion represents

31

your mission, drive, interests, and your "why". The profitable market reflects the market's demand for your offer—people who are willing to pay for your products or services.

The overlap between your passion, expertise, and profitable market is your "Profit Spot," also known as your "perfect niche." This is where you find profitable opportunities for your business.

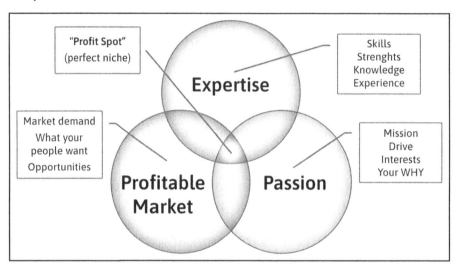

By identifying your Profit Spot, you can create a business that aligns with your passions and expertise while meeting your ideal clients' needs.

If you've been hesitant to narrow down your niche, let's explore how it can benefit your business.

My definition of a **niche is providing a specific solution to a specific problem your ideal audience struggles with**.

The key here is to be as specific as possible by identifying your one hot area of expertise and choosing one well-defined group of ideal clients you want to serve by solving a specific problem they have.

You may be tempted to resist narrowing your focus, thinking you can help everyone or that your method works for any person in any situation. It's especially challenging when you have a lot of special gifts and talents… when you can do so many things well, and you love doing all of them. It might feel like any time you narrow the scope of what you offer by focusing on a specific audience or specific subset of your skills, you leave money on the table.

In reality, the opposite is true. By trying to be everything to everyone, you run the risk of being unappealing to anyone. While trying not to limit ourselves, we are actually making it challenging for those around us to understand what we do, promote us, and refer to us.

When you hone in on your niche, you can establish yourself as an expert in your field and attract the right clients who are eager for the specific solution you offer.

I know this from personal experience.

When I first started my photography business, I felt like I had hit the jackpot; it was the perfect combination of my skills and passion.

I poured my heart and soul into creating a website that showcased all the different types of photography I was capable of, from family portraits to boudoir sessions to product shots. At one point, I was proud to list 17(!) different types of services, because I believed that offering a wide range of packages was the key to attracting clients.

But as the weeks went by, I realized something wasn't working. Despite offering a wide variety of imaginative photography services, I struggled to get clients, and I couldn't understand why.

I was starting to feel like a failure.

One day, as I was attending a networking event and trying to entice businesswomen to sign up for a luxury glamor session, someone asked me if I did headshots. I scoffed at the idea—headshots were so basic, and they didn't require all the creative skills I had. But as I heard the question again and again, something clicked.

I realized that I had been so focused on what I wanted to offer that I hadn't been listening to what people actually needed and wanted. This was a huge turning point for me—I finally heard what my ideal clients were interested in buying.

I decided to niche down and focus solely on headshots for entrepreneurs.

At first, I was scared. I didn't want to be labeled as "just a headshot photographer." I had so much more to offer! But as I put all my energy into this one area, something miraculous happened: people started paying attention. They were interested in my work, and soon, daily referrals and inquiries about working with me became the norm.

I had become known as a specialist—the go-to photographer for business headshots and marketing photography. And the best part? I was doing what I loved and making a living from it.

I learned that when it comes to starting a business, less is more. By focusing on the needs of my clients, I was able to build a profitable business.

In just a few months, I became the highest-paid headshot photographer in town, with clients flying in from out of state to work with me. My calendar was fully booked, and I broke the six-figure mark.

Do you see how this success came only after I found my Profit Spot—when I focused on *one* hot area of expertise and chose *one* well-defined group of ideal clients I wanted to serve by solving a *specific problem* they had?

The truth is, when you focus on a specific niche, you open up doors to more opportunities for success and profit in your business!

Once you operate from your Profit Spot, it becomes easier to stand out in a crowded market, own your expertise, create hot-selling offers, find ideal clients, and market and promote your services with ease.

Are you ready to find your Profit Spot?

Exercise 6: Find Your Profit Spot

Initially, we examined your expertise from a general and overarching viewpoint rather than focusing on specific solutions you offer.

After completing Exercise #5, you should have a list of up to three areas that fall within your "sweet spot," where your passion overlaps with your expertise.

Get a fresh sheet of paper and write your first area of expertise across the top.

As an example, I'll use "getting clients online," one of my areas of expertise.

As you can probably tell, it's very general and broad, so we have some work ahead of us.

To start with, we need to identify our ideal audience and be as specific as we can.

In my case, I could simply say that my audience is business owners, but that's still not specific enough. We need to narrow it down more.

I could choose gender and age. I primarily work with women between the ages of 40 and 70.

Another aspect I could consider is where they are in their business journey. Are they just starting out, been in business for a while, or been running a successful business for many years (primarily offline)?

I could also examine the revenue generated by their company. For instance, I mostly work with individuals who have been in business for three to five years but haven't yet achieved success online and haven't broken six figures.

Do you see how you need to get very specific about your audience?

Now, it's your turn. On your paper, write down a detailed description of your ideal client. Who would benefit the most from this specific expertise? It helps to imagine them as a real person you know.

Here are some sample questions to help you focus:

- Who is your ideal client?

- What age range does your ideal client fall into?

- What is their gender?

- What is their occupation?

- What is their ethnicity?

- Are they married or single?

- Do they have children?

- What is their income level?

- What is their education level?

- What are their hobbies and interests?

- What are their values and beliefs?

- Where do they live?

- What is their cultural background?

- What is their family situation?

- What are their goals and aspirations?

- What motivates them?

- What do they dream about?

- Who are their heroes?

- What common misconceptions or false beliefs do they hold?

- What are their personality traits?

- What is their daily routine?

- How do they feel about their business (career, relationships, health, finances, spiritual or personal growth)?

Take your time and describe your ideal client for this area of your expertise. You don't need to answer all of the questions above—just the ones that help you paint a clear picture of your ideal audience. And you can, of course, add your own.

Next, we are going to look at what your ideal clients struggle with. We need to ensure that the area of expertise you plan to focus on is something that addresses your ideal client's challenges, and something they are willing to invest in it to overcome them.

Here are some questions you must be able to answer about your ideal clients:

- What isn't currently working in their lives (personal or professional)?

- What are their biggest obstacles or challenges?

- What frustrates them about their current situation?

- What are the symptoms or discomforts they are experiencing?

- What is it costing them?

- What do they want to overcome, eliminate, or resolve?

- What have they tried in the past to address their biggest pain points?

- Have they invested money in resolving these challenges?

- How long have they struggled with these issues?

- What's one thing your ideal clients desire the most?

- What do they want to create or experience?

When responding to these questions, it's crucial to put

yourself in your ideal clients' shoes and describe their experiences from their point of view, using their language and their words. Focus on the challenges that they recognize as problems and are already actively trying to solve.

For example, in my case, my ideal clients feel overwhelmed by conflicting advice from various experts and coaches. They are frustrated that even though they are seemingly doing everything right, they are not getting the results they want. They often question the direction of their business, their message, and their marketing approach.

Their biggest challenge is getting clients on a consistent basis. They invest considerable time, effort, and money in solutions, programs, trainings, and coaches in order to create a profitable business and prove to themselves and loved ones that they have what it takes.

The key is to make it easy for your ideal clients to recognize themselves and their struggles in your description.

Take a moment to brainstorm all of the challenges your ideal clients struggle with AND are willing to invest in to overcome. This exercise will help you determine whether there is a profitable market for this specific expertise.

If you have identified multiple areas of expertise in the Sweet Spot exercise, repeat Exercise 6 for each of these areas.

After completing the exercises, evaluate which of your areas of expertise holds the greatest potential for profitability. This specific expertise will be your focus from now on.

Besides narrowing down your expertise to the most profitable one, you now should be clear on the *specific audience* you'll be focusing on, and a *specific problem* your ideal clients have.

Now, it's time to identify the *specific solution* that addresses their most significant challenge and helps them achieve their desired results.

Profitable Niche

With a clear understanding of your ideal clients' needs and the unique value you bring to the table, you can create an irresistible offer that solves their problems and delivers results.

The key to keep in mind here is that you want to be very clear on multiple solutions you can provide, and choose one at a time to focus on, until you establish yourself as an expert in that specific niche.

Exercise 7: Define Your Niche

Let's once again look at an example of my audience: women entrepreneurs who struggle to get clients online.

Based on my unique expertise, skills, and background, here are just some of the things I can offer my clients:

- How to get clients online with free five-day challenges

- How to get clients online using Facebook groups

- How to get clients online using live broadcasts

- How to get clients online with virtual events and workshops

I could also focus my solution on teaching specific skills

that would help them to get clients online faster and more effectively.

- For example, I can teach my ideal clients how to create: Client-attracting marketing materials

- Irresistible lead magnets

- Joint Venture partnerships

- Simple funnels

- Leveraged online programs

As you can see, all of these ideas fall under the broad category of "getting clients online," but each one is a well-defined, stand-alone solution that meets a specific need.

Now, it's your turn to brainstorm specific solutions that fall into your chosen area of expertise. Set a goal to come up with at least five ideas, but don't be surprised if you end up with 10 or 20, considering you're working with a topic that is in your sweet spot, where your zone of genius meets your passion.

Now comes the challenging part—choosing just ONE of these solutions.

This is often one of the toughest aspects of defining your niche. Remember, it's not about having a narrow business approach; it's about narrowing down the first offer you want to be known for.

To become a recognized go-to expert in your field and achieve success, you must choose just ONE solution and focus on it for at least a year.

Trust me; you'll be amazed at the results you'll achieve if

41

you stay committed.

Take a good look at all the solutions you brainstormed, and circle the one you'd like to choose as your niche.

Got one? Fantastic!

You now have your perfect niche—a *specific solution* to a *specific problem* that your *specific audience* is searching for.

Exercise 8: Perfect Niche Test

Let's do a Perfect Niche Test to ensure you're on the right track.

Ask yourself these questions about the niche you've just chosen:

1. Do you consider yourself an expert in this niche?

2. Are you passionate about this niche?

3. Will you be happy if you become widely known for this niche? Ideally, you should be feeling anticipation and excitement when you think about this happening.

4. Are your ideal clients aware of the problem you are solving? Do they know they have this challenge or issue?

5. Are they actively searching for solutions and paying money to solve this problem?

6. Are there competitors who solve this problem? Having competitors is actually a good thing, especially if they are successful. It means people are willing to invest in solutions around this topic.

7. Are you solving one problem and one problem only? Make sure you are focusing on one specific solution to just one problem they have. Don't try to address all challenges in one offer.

8. Are you clear on tangible and measurable results your solution provides?

9. Are you willing to commit to this niche for the next year?

10. Does this niche align with your long-term vision and goals for your business?

Congratulations if you answered YES to all ten questions! You've successfully defined your niche, which is a significant achievement. Few business owners go through this process and achieve the level of clarity you have reached. Well done! This newfound focus will open up a world of opportunities for you.

But what if you answered NO to one or more of these questions?

Don't worry; it's not a dead end. Go back to the list of specific solutions you created and see if another niche might be a better fit for you. Refining your niche is an iterative process, so don't be afraid to make adjustments as you go along. Just be sure to go through the Perfect Niche Test questions again! Remember, clarity is key to achieving success, and staying committed to this process will pay off in the long run.

How are you feeling now? Are you ready to confidently own your expertise and start sharing it with the world?

It's time to let everyone know about it—from friends and

family to potential clients—because the more people who know about your unique skills and solutions, the more visible you are, and the greater your potential for success.

As a plus, having a clear niche makes it easier to tailor your messaging to your audience, so you can effectively communicate the unique value you offer.

Let's put this into practice by considering how easily you can now answer the question, "What do you do?"

By following this simple template and using the answers you've generated for your niche, you can craft a specific and clear response:

"I work with (your ideal audience) who struggle with (the specific problem you solve) by (specific solution you provide)."

For instance, my response might be: "I work with business owners who struggle with getting clients online by helping them create and sell profitable online programs."

Take a few minutes to write down your own "what do you do statement" based on your chosen niche.

And remember, owning and claiming your expertise is about being proud of what sets you apart from others. It's not about bragging or comparing yourself to other people. It's about embracing who you are and what you have to offer. Don't hold back—shine a light on your expertise and let the world see and hear what you have to offer.

By taking full ownership of your expertise, you'll be able to attract more clients, confidently charge higher rates for your services, get more referrals, and build your business faster.

But what's the next step after you've claimed your niche and expertise?

Well, it's time to figure out how to leverage and monetize your skills. In other words, you need to decide what type of offer you'll make to your ideal clients.

For an expertise-based business, the most common paid offers include:

- One-on-one coaching

- Done-for-you services

- Done-with-you services

- VIP days

- Group coaching

- Retreats

- Workshops

- Events

- Memberships

- Masterminds

- Online programs

Out of all of these offers, the least leveraged and scalable is one-on-one coaching, and the most leveraged is… you've probably guessed—online programs.

A leveraged online program is your recorded knowledge, expertise, and experience on a certain topic packaged in a way that makes it easy for people to access, consume, and use it to get results… without any access to you! This means that with an online program, you can reach a broader audience and scale your business without sacrificing your time and energy.

Creating an online program is the absolute best way to leverage and showcase your expertise, and I sincerely hope that you'll see it as the next step on your journey of creating successful and profitable expertise-based business.

If you'd like to learn more about how to take those next steps, I highly recommend that you take a look at my other three books in this series: *Teach Your Expertise*, *Leverage Your Expertise*, and *Monetize Your Expertise*.

But before you do, turn the page for real-life stories from other entrepreneurs who've taken steps to own their expertise and build a fulfilling business. They'll show you what's possible when you have the courage and determination to take the leap and find your profitable niche.

It's completely possible for you to take control of your own life and build the business of your dreams! I've done it. My clients have done it. And you can do it, too. I hope by reading their stories, you find the inspiration and determination to claim and monetize your expertise.

And don't forget…

This book comes with free gifts, exercises, and resources from each of the contributing authors. You can access all of them on the bonus Resources Page:

OwnYourExpertiseBook.com/gifts

Chapter 3
Turning Adversity into Opportunity:
A Voyage of Insight and Empowerment
by Florence Callender

The day I found out my daughter couldn't read was the worst day of my life.

At the end of her second grade, I was summoned to a meeting with her teacher and school principal. After the usual greetings and pleasantries, I was told that she would have to be held back a year because she could not read. Being a speech therapist in a different school, I was shocked and embarrassed by this news. I asked them to hold off on the final decision and give me the summer to do some work with her. They agreed.

After delving into tireless online research and scouring through our local library shelves, a single word kept popping up: *dyslexia*. I quickly connected with a dyslexia specialist who found that—yes! — my darling girl did indeed have it.

Reflecting on that fateful meeting in the principal's office, I realized that the school was not equipped to accommodate my daughter's needs, so I took control of her education. I attended a four-day training on how to work with children with dyslexia and improve their reading, spelling, attention, and focus, among other things. I was determined to give her the best chance at success. Thus, I worked with her tirelessly over that entire summer.

So, while most children spent the greater part of their vacation time playing, my daughter was using tools, techniques, and strategies I discovered to build on what the dyslexia evaluator had told me. Our hard work paid off, and by the end of the summer, she had made significant progress. When she returned to school in September and was retested, she was promoted to the third grade.

With knowledge and understanding comes power; I was now equipped to seek ways to support her on her journey toward success.

I continued studying and took more than 10 different courses on dyslexia, read scores of books, and attended dozens of workshops and seminars. I worked with various tools and used different techniques with my daughter. I retained the things that worked for her and disregarded the ones that didn't seem to make a difference. I kept testing and implementing new things, watching videos, and learning new techniques and strategies. She went on to excel and become one of the brightest students in her class. When she finished high school, she graduated as the valedictorian!

On her graduation day, as I gazed at my daughter walking across the stage in her simple but elegant dress to give her speech, a mosaic of memories flooded my mind... from that first day in the principal's office advocating for her educational needs, to sending countless messages and videos about dyslexia to teachers to preparing her for weekend reading assignments at our church. That moment was a tangible testament to all our hard work paying off!

Her self-esteem had skyrocketed. As for me, I realized that my feelings of *overwhelm*, *helplessness*, and *fear* had been replaced by *contentment, confidence,* and a liberating *peace of mind* about her future.

After her graduation, other parents who knew about her challenges kept coming to me asking what I had done to turn her academic journey around. I felt compelled to share my knowledge and experience freely whenever I was invited to do so. I met parents who thought it was the school's responsibility to teach their children and make them learn, and others who were afraid to work independently with their children at home because they had no formal training or certification in teaching or tutoring.

When I first started helping my daughter, I had no knowledge of dyslexia. I just wanted to help her do well. But through my trainings, I found out that dyslexia is the most common learning difference seen in schools.

From my experience with my daughter, I learned that:

- You don't have to depend on the school.

- There are no secrets tucked away for people with special certificates.

- Every parent can learn to help their child.

- I was developing a deep knowledge around how to help children with dyslexia.

I became so passionate about helping other parents deliver their children from the prison of "teaching disabilities" and incorrect learning perspectives I saw in the schools where I worked that I helped regardless of whether or not they paid me.

In 2018, I decided to leave the school system and subcontract my services to an educational agency to evaluate children's speech and language abilities. As I tested them in their homes, I felt the conviction building inside me, like a wave rising from the depths, until it crashed upon the shore of my consciousness with a thunderous roar: *working on my own terms, free from the cookie-cutter approach of the system, would enable me to better assist the parents I encountered.*

I've never doubted my ability to inspire and teach others. Being an educator is simply who I am. I have this special talent for breaking down complex ideas and making them easily understandable. The fact that I receive invitations to speak at different events like school graduations, church services, and educational and women's conferences only confirms that my message has truly connected with a lot of people.

While I never saw myself as an official dyslexia specialist nor received any special education on it, I became adept at recognizing its signs. My desire to share my knowledge and assist others propelled me to embrace my expertise, combine my speech pathology skills with this newfound knowledge, and reach out to a wider audience. **I felt a strong urge to empower others and create a meaningful, positive influence in their lives.**

So, I took a leap of faith and launched my own business. Much to my joy, my dyslexic daughter followed suit and established her own enterprise, bringing her remarkable technology skills to the table. She now works side by side with me!

Around this time, I also learned about and attended Alina Vincent's High Profit Programs (HPP) live event… an online workshop that teaches participants how to create a program based on their knowledge, experience, and expertise.

Perhaps it was our common background in academia, Alina's style of presenting, or her effortless, instantaneous, solutions to the questions asked and challenges presented; whatever it was, I resonated with Alina and enrolled in her year-long Rising Stars Mastermind with the goal of creating a program to help parents of dyslexic children do what I had done for my daughter.

As I followed the framework and structure Alina provided to create my online program, I was forced to organize the things I had learned and determine how I could present them in a format that would benefit parents and give them tangible outcomes.

Being a member of Alina's mastermind group was a profoundly transformative experience that allowed me to passionately share my dedication to assisting parents. It served as a powerful reminder of how easily we underestimate the value of our own knowledge and contributions. The unwavering affirmations, uplifting encouragement, and priceless advice from fellow members opened my eyes to my true worth in helping parents and the tremendous opportunities I have to positively impact the lives of thousands of children with my expertise.

Since my journey with Alina began in the summer of 2021, I have created and launched:

- A five-week program... *Learning Made Easy: Success Secrets for Parenting Dyslexia.*

- A five-day mini course... *Reading Made Easy: 5-Day Boost.*

- A one-hour video course... *Brain Hacks to Accelerate*

Your Child's learning.

- A masterclass… *3 Unintended Mistakes Parents Make that Keep Their Children Struggling to Read, Learn, and Do Homework.*

- Three free reports for parents of children with reading and learning difficulties.

Plus, I'm currently developing a one-on-one coaching program and five-day spelling challenge, as well as working on a giveaway and free summit.

As a parent, you dream of supporting your child on their path to success. But what happens when your child is faced with challenges in reading and learning, and you don't know what steps to take next?

When Monique and Esther discovered my online program, they felt hopeful that they had finally found the support they needed to navigate their children's learning difficulties.

Monique's daughter struggled in school and was resistant to homework. Monique was stressed out and at her wits end. As she worked through my Learning Made Easy program, she began to see changes in her daughter's attitude toward schoolwork. By the end of the program, the fighting disappeared, and Monique's daughter had found joy in learning.

Esther, on the other hand, felt lost and frustrated before starting the Learning Made Easy program. She had been trying different strategies to help her daughter with her spelling and reading. Nothing was helping. After working through my program, she gained clear direction on how to help her daughter learn. Her daughter even achieved her first-ever 100% on a spelling test, much to the joy of her entire family.

The overarching message of hope and inspiration that these stories convey is that *parents can make a significant difference in their children's lives*. They can help them succeed in school and beyond, no matter the challenges. All it takes is the right tools and guidance, and that's exactly what my program provides.

The benefits of the Learning Made Easy program extend beyond helping children. By providing parents with support and the resources they need, **I create a ripple effect that improves their own mental health and well-being**, making it easier for them to support their child effectively.

According to the National Center for Education Statistics, 65 percent of fourth graders in the United States are not proficient in reading. This doesn't have to be. Parents do not have to depend on teachers or anyone else to teach their children how to read. I proved that by successfully helping my daughter at home. And that's why I'm obsessed with helping parents of children with reading and learning challenges pave the way for their learning success.

I knew this new knowledge was important and worked, so I started integrating it in my work as a speech therapist and saw significant results. This showed me that you *can* build on what you know, become an expert at it, and make money from it. But even after owning my expertise, I had trouble marketing it because of money blocks.

Here are some steps I took to own and monetize my expertise:

- **I recognized the true value of my expertise.** I researched my niche and looked at similar programs being offered and their price points. As I reflected on the experience of taking my daughter from failure to success, I realized and acknowledged the unique perspective and insights I bring to the table. This shift helped me realize the impact my expertise can have on others.

- **I reframed my mindset.** Moving from thinking like a speech therapist to an entrepreneur was a tough journey, but I knew it was critical for my success. I knew that what schools offer is not enough to help children with learning differences. When doubts and negative thoughts arose, I challenged them by questioning their validity and looking to evidence for the truth. By staying consistent in this practice, I evolved my mindset and gained a more positive and confident outlook. It wasn't easy, but I proved to myself that anything is possible when you believe in yourself and push past your limitations.

- **I did the hard work.** After owning my expertise, I monetized it through diligent efforts. With the foundational elements in place, I priced my program so it balanced accessibility and reflected the value of my expertise. I also shifted my mindset about social media, building an email list, crafting compelling content, and seeking potential partners for program promotion.

To help you own your expertise, too, here are three actionable tips:

1. **Find a mentor or coach** who has already achieved success in what you want to do. Learn from their experience and get insights into what works.

2. **Develop a detailed plan** that includes all the aspects

of market research, creating content, marketing, and running a program.

3. **Stay committed to your goals and keep moving forward with your plan**, even when obstacles arise… as they will. Believe in yourself and your expertise and be willing to invest the time and effort necessary to make your program a success!

My passion lies in helping parents of children who are struggling to read discover how to navigate the intersection of parenting and education with confidence and ease, turn academic challenges into opportunities for growth and achievement, and watch their child soar.

Pushing past my own self-doubt and limiting beliefs about my expertise allowed me to create a profitable online program. This journey taught me three essential lessons that have bolstered my business growth, amplified my income, and boosted my confidence as an authority in my industry.

Lesson 1: When it comes to business matters, I know more than I give myself credit for.

After working in academia for over 25 years, I thought my lack of business experience was an insurmountable obstacle to succeeding online. Yet upon closer inspection, I discovered that a lifetime of being a school-based speech therapist and learning specialist had given me the necessary skill set not just to help my dyslexic daughter, but to also launch something that meets a real need in the world.

Lesson 2: People respect me and think highly of what I do.

After I embraced my expertise and launched my online

program, it was clear that people truly respected me. The outpouring of positivity served as a reminder that by not believing in myself enough, I had been shortchanging what others think about me. All their feedback demonstrated just how much they valued my expertise! That realization spurred a newfound confidence to market myself as I recognized how much I have to offer.

Lesson 3: People recognize the value of my expertise and are willing to invest in it.

Often, we underestimate the value of our skills and talents. Initially, when I developed my online program to assist children with dyslexia, I doubted its marketability due to the existence of numerous similar programs. However, upon engaging with potential participants, I discovered their desire for a high-quality, customized solution specifically tailored to their child, rather than a generic offering. This realization provided me with the confidence to launch my program.

Embracing these three lessons has had a significant impact on my business. I believe in myself and my work more. I am not scared to publicize what I do anymore.

Creating a salable online program was a game-changer for me. Now, I am excited to see what happens next!

Reflecting on my journey as a learning specialist and entrepreneur, there are three crucial insights I wish I had known about myself and my expertise before embarking on this business endeavor.

1. The value I bring stems from my knowledge, experience, and expertise, transcending any specific industry boundaries. It is the unique combination of these qual-

ities that sets me apart and allows me to make a meaningful impact.

2. My passion is an unstoppable force, fueling my drive to overcome obstacles and reach new heights of success. With unwavering resilience and commitment, I have the power to rise to the top, surmounting any challenges that come my way.

3. Embracing continuous growth and learning is essential. By staying open to new insights, honing my skills, and adapting to evolving trends, I am better equipped to thrive in an ever-changing landscape. This mindset of ongoing improvement propels me forward, ensuring my success and expanding my ability to serve parents and make a lasting difference in the lives of children.

If you're contemplating the path of owning your expertise and using it to serve others, I have a message for you:

Release any preconceived notions and dismiss any self-doubt that may arise. Instead, set your intention high, craft a well-defined plan, and unleash your full potential to conquer the goals you have set for yourself!

Embrace the limitless possibilities that await you on this path of self-discovery and service. With untiring determination and unwavering belief in your abilities, you have the power to surpass your own expectations and create a profound impact on the lives of others.

There is no limit to what you can accomplish!

What are you waiting for?

Florence Callender helps parents work with their struggling children, so they learn faster and easier, have a better school experience, and succeed in life. She has over 25 years of experience working with students who have learning differences and helped her own dyslexic daughter go from failing in second grade to graduating valedictorian of her high school class. Florence is a speech-language pathologist and brain-based learning specialist, the founder of Innovative Lifestyle Solutions, and the creator of Learning Made Easy: Success Secrets for Parenting Dyslexia. She helps people discover tools and strategies to position their child for long-term learning success. You can learn more about her here: https://www.FlorenceCallender.com.

Get Florence's free gift…

Unlock Your Child's Potential: 4 Brain Hacks Every Parent Should Know to promote optimal brain development in your child and improve their cognitive abilities and academic success, here:

OwnYourExpertiseBook.com/gifts

Chapter 4
Small Shifts, Big Impacts:
Harnessing the Power of Expertise
by Tricia Conyers

In the fast-paced and ever-evolving world we live in, there is little doubt that owning your expertise has become an important part of shaping a fulfilling and inspiring life.

As I reflect on my own journey of transitioning from a long and successful career in the corporate world to starting my own business, I have learned valuable lessons about embracing and leveraging my expertise to create meaningful impact for myself and for others.

Finding Possibility in Confusion

Over the past two decades, my professional journey encompassed a range of roles, from change agent to coach to trainer to learning architect and more.

My corporate career offered me ample and exciting opportunities for growth, challenge, and continuous learning. My changing roles and expanding challenges stretched my limits and encouraged personal and professional growth. I was a fully dedicated member of my team and organization. I had worked my way to a senior leadership position and established a reputation of being capable of contributing both breadth and depth of knowledge and experience in the change industry.

However, as the years passed, I started to question the boundaries of my career.

What would the next decade hold? Could I continue to

find growth opportunities, inspiration, and purpose if I remained where I was?

Where I once found excitement and opportunity in my career and role, it now began to feel repetitive.

The once-thriving opportunities for personal and professional development now felt more scarce, leaving me questioning my sense of purpose.

I wondered, "What could be next? What might lay beyond the horizon of familiarity? What might happen if I stepped into an unknown space?"

As the world underwent profound shifts in 2020, I too experienced a personal shift: *a desire to contribute and add value beyond what I was currently doing.*

Months turned into a ceaseless cycle of deliberation as I weighed the risks and rewards of a significant career change.

The cultivated reputation and security of my established corporate career built upon years of dedicated effort stood in stark contrast to the leap of faith required to forge a path as an entrepreneur.

In the face of this uncertainty, I found myself on the threshold of what was and what could be.

I was apprehensive of an unpredictable and unclear future.

Leaving the organization I had faithfully served for two decades felt disloyal, and starting a business felt overwhelmingly risky, albeit exciting.

I knew that starting a business would require patience,

determination, and resilience. I knew it was going to challenge me in ways I had not previously experienced, and I had many doubts about my readiness for a successful solo career.

Despite this tension, I held onto a belief that I had valuable experience to offer others. I wanted to share it in a way that empowered me to shape a life I loved, doing work that inspired me!

I believed I could have a career that would provide flexibility, challenge, inspiration, and security.

I was teetering between contemplation and taking the first step. I was standing on the edge of change.

Patience as a Catalyst for Change

In January 2022, I resigned from the corporate world.

The first challenge of the entrepreneurial path came upon me quickly.

Communication.

I needed to be able to articulate my expertise—the real value I could provide to potential clients—succinctly and concisely.

I struggled to summarize how I could help clients in a captivating way.

The diverse range of expertise I had acquired over the years made it difficult to condense into a concise elevator pitch.

I knew the importance of making a compelling first impression to establish firm footing and gain momentum.

This would be the very first of the "knowing, doing" challenges that I faced in my journey—the type of challenge where you know what action you need to take, but you struggle to take the action successfully.

I had so much to offer my potential clients.

During the decades I'd worked in my corporate job, I'd led change programs that delivered breakthrough performance results, developed work teams into high-performing teams, advanced the confidence and capabilities of hundreds of leaders, delivered professional development interventions on many topics, and designed and facilitated environments wherein people thought differently, collaborated more effectively, and unleashed new wisdom.

How does a person sum up all of that in a way that piques curiosity and resonates with others?

Did I focus on a single area, or be more general?

Honing in and distilling my essence—**owning my expertise**—was proving to be a process.

I spent hours pondering the "right" answer and lamenting over failed conversations to communicate in a captivating way.

I knew that the precious few seconds of an introduction held immense power, and that I wasn't doing my best.

Looking back, I have come to appreciate the value of patience when facing these defining questions.

Luckily, the discomfort that accompanies uncertainty is the space where new ideas and solutions take root and flourish… where growth occurs.

Through introspection and self-reflection, I gradually began to connect with what I wanted to do versus what I could do.

This reframing encouraged creativity, and I began to feel inspired and motivated as I focused on what brought out the best in me and what brought me joy.

It was through this process that my answer to the question "What do you do?" started to emerge.

The Power of Purposeful Positioning and Allies

I discovered that by helping others lead differently, I could bring inspiration, excitement, possibility, success, and results to their work and teams.

I wanted to help leaders find and leverage the many day-to-day leadership moments at their disposal to motivate others, inspire action, and shape their own leadership style.

As I set out to create the first of my online programs to help leaders lead differently, I knew I could not do it alone.

I needed the support and guidance of allies who believed in my vision and could offer valuable insights, direction, and expertise.

Alina Vincent's High Profit Programs live event gave me a head start in terms of structuring my own online program and understanding the process, mindset, and marketing required to bring it to life.

Through the process of developing that first program, I gained further clarity about how I could help clients reframe the way they viewed basic components of their businesses and make small changes that would lead to big results.

This first program focused on the most often overlooked leadership moment: meetings.

Meetings are key business interventions and leadership moments; they're opportunities for leaders to inspire action, shape team culture, and drive performance.

But if we're being honest, while many leaders view meetings as a necessary gathering during which to communicate and check in with team members, team members often view them as disruptions that interrupt important work.

In my **Lead Meetings That Work** program, I help leaders utilize meetings as an opportunity to finesse their leadership style, drive results, and excite and empower their teams.

How Small Shifts Deliver Big Impacts

Shaping, creating, and launching this program has been a rewarding experience.

It has been an opportunity for me to role model how to lead differently, and I've experienced firsthand how small shifts can have big impacts on individual confidence, team performance, and organizational culture. These small shifts can be a tipping point for change in companies.

This is in stark contrast to typical extensive leadership programs that are difficult to translate into practical day-to-day interventions.

From a quantitative perspective, the numbers speak for themselves. I've enrolled more than 60 leaders across dozens of companies and generated substantial revenue from coaching and programs. It's also been motivating to see the steadily growing listener base of my *Every Little Mode* podcast, and to have multiple new leadership programs in development.

However, the true reward came from the personal growth and development I witnessed in the leaders I worked with.

The program served as a catalyst for their leadership confidence, empowering them to finesse and own their leadership styles.

This newfound confidence had a ripple effect on team performance and the overall culture within organizations.

One such example is Ashleigh, the owner of BIOSTRAT JV, an Oil and Gas Service Provider, who experienced a profound shift in her leadership approach through Lead Meetings That Work.

She shared how the program transformed her leadership style, overall performance, and team culture.

The program enabled her to create space for collaboration and contributions from her team, resulting in higher engagement and happiness among her team members.

Here's what she had to say after completing the Lead Meetings That Work program:

"Before participating in the Lead Meetings That Work program, I took a very hands-on approach to my leadership role in my business. While I was effective in setting a strong example, I was not encouraging enough collaboration and contributions from my team.

"This program has taught me how to use my meetings to create space for team members to have a voice and for me

to encourage and acknowledge their suggestions. This shift has not only transformed my meetings, but has also changed my leadership style, improved our overall performance, and enhanced our team culture. My team is now more engaged and happier in their work, which is a testament to the power of this program.

"Every manager wants more contributions and engagement from their team, but it can be challenging to know how to do this. This program has given me the guidance and strategies I need to lead in a way that brings out the best in my team. I highly recommend this program to anyone looking to elevate not only their meeting leadership skills, but also their overall leadership style and drive success in their business."

Results Are More Than Just Numbers

As I reflect on my journey, it hasn't been without obstacles and doubts.

There were moments when I questioned my decision to leave the corporate world and take on challenges that tested my belief in myself. But there is a thrill from taking on new experiences.

I recognized that doubt is a natural companion when pursuing new goals.

I've had to make many mindset shifts on my journey, and I anticipate having to make more as I continue.

Rather than letting doubt stop me from pursuing the creation of an inspiring life and business, I acknowledge it and move on.

Belief is the single most critical factor in business—and perhaps in life.

68

I learned to redefine failure as a necessary outcome on the path to success, and I remained open to experimenting, seeking help, and trusting the process.

If you're failing, you're on the right track!

Failing means you are taking action, making progress, learning, and being committed.

I've learned to acknowledge the failures and trust the process, ask for help, and experiment.

I've also learned the importance of slowing down, taking pause, and allowing space to think.

If you're constantly caught up in the activity of doing (which is common for so many of us), there's no space to make connections or to reflect on whether you're doing the right thing (versus doing everything).

If there is one tip I could offer, it would be to find yourself a thinking partner, and practice weekly thinking sessions.

For me, taking time to speak my thoughts out loud in the presence of a trusted and attentive listener has unlocked my own wisdom.

Plus, it encourages me to take a short pause to reconnect with purpose and reconsider whether my activities align with it.

There are many other lessons that have stood out for me along this journey.

I discovered the importance of finding work that energizes and fulfills me, aligning my activities with my purpose.

I also learned to be patient and kind with myself.

The process of creation, discovery, and becoming is not a straight line or a planned and organized process.

Finally, I've experienced how difficult it is to recognize when we're holding ourselves back!

Get help, support, and coaching; find people who can help you spot your own limiting beliefs, see alternate paths, and define new possibilities.

Through Island Inspirations, it's my mission to help others use day-to-day moments to "lead differently"—to help leaders ignite energy, passion, and action within their teams.

I believe that by inspiring others to embrace new ideas, we can create a ripple effect of positive change.

In closing, I'd like to share one of my favorite quotes, by Ralph Waldo Emerson: *"The mind, once stretched by a new idea, never returns to its original dimensions."*

This quote encapsulates the essence of my business and the power of embracing new ideas and perspectives.

I hope that you, too, find possibility in these ideas.

Tricia Conyers is a leadership coach, facilitator, trainer, and podcaster. She helps individuals and teams to unlock their full potential and achieve breakthrough results. Through a combination of one-on-one coaching, hybrid professional development programs, facilitated in-person experiential events, and her Every Little Model podcast, she helps leaders to think differently, recognize and leverage leadership moments, and develop the confidence and capabilities they need to succeed in today's fast-paced business world. You can learn more about her here: https://islandinspirations.co/.

Get Tricia's free gift…

15 Meeting Leadership Tips to help you lead more effective, engaging, productive meetings, here:

https://OwnYourExpertiseBook.com/gifts

Chapter 5
Creating a New Life: One Business at a Time
by Nedra Wendel

In 2010, I was struggling emotionally, living paycheck to paycheck, and feeling like I was about the worst version of myself I could be. I was working as a hotel manager, and by everyone else's standards, was quite successful in my job. But most days, I found myself angry and stressed out.

I was also married and a mom to two beautiful teenage daughters. I should have been enjoying life. Instead, I felt guilty for not being the best mom and wife I could be.

I kept thinking, *what is wrong with me?*

I didn't know. Nor could I see any other options. This was just the way life was.

And just when I thought it couldn't get any worse, it did.

The owners of the hotel I worked for sold the business, and my already stressful job became unbearable with the transition to new ownership.

That's when I decided *I had to make a change.*

I couldn't see it or understand it at the time, but my life was being course corrected.

I finally became motivated to explore my options and take action.

Finding a different job I was qualified for and making the same salary seemed highly unlikely.

So, I figured if I couldn't find a new job, I'd make one.

I started asking people, including business owners, in my community what kind of new business our town needed. Nearly everyone I spoke with wanted a fitness center. While I didn't have any fitness experience, I did know how to manage a business.

However, I didn't think I had enough skills or the expertise to do it alone. Going with a franchise seemed the best option.

It was one of the most challenging things I've ever done. I had to dig deep and learn how to do things I'd never done before, like make a business plan, calculate build-out and start-up budgets, and create a pro forma (a financial projection of estimated expenses and revenue).

Six banks turned me down, and each rejection was hard to take.

But that didn't stop me. I couldn't let it stop me.

I was determined to make it happen.

I kept repeating my mantra, "I will find a way. There is no other option."

I *did* find a way, and that's when everything started to change!

In 2011, I opened my first fitness center franchise.

Stepping into being a business owner pushed me to grow in ways I couldn't have imagined. Instead of receiving a regular paycheck, my performance determined my livelihood. I had to become a new version of myself, so I dug into personal development to uplevel. It became a way of life.

I didn't realize the significance of my personal growth then, but I was becoming ME… someone I now love, respect, and cherish.

For the next two years, life was going great, to the point where I opened a second location and was working on launching the third. I loved owning and operating the fitness centers. Plus, I was living a much healthier lifestyle, eating nutritious foods and exercising on a regular basis.

Then I got news a mother never wants to hear.

I discovered my then 18-year-old daughter had an eating disorder.

I was crushed. *How could this be?*

When I looked at her, all I saw was a beautiful young woman who had so much going for her.

Why couldn't she see what I saw? How could she hate her body?

As reality sunk in, my childhood memories came rushing back…

… the struggle with my own weight and being made fun of for being the "fat kid."

I grew up watching the women in my life grapple with their weight. In fact, I even remember having weight-loss challenges (or competitions) with my mother, grandmother, and older cousin when I was just 10 years old. My heart sank every time I stepped onto the scale.

Worrying about my weight and dieting became a normal way of life.

What had I taught my daughter about food, dieting, and body image?

I could clearly see the generational patterns. I had become accustomed to this way of living, but now that I could see the effects it had on my daughter, I knew *it had to stop*.

This way of life was no longer acceptable, and I made the decision to find the solution.

Much like opening my first franchise, I didn't know how I was going to make this major shift, but I *had to* find the way.

My sole focus was on helping my daughter.

I didn't know it at the time, but as I embarked on a mission to heal my daughter, it became my healing journey for ME.

And my life completely transformed, revealing a deeper purpose within me.

With renewed focus, I started exploring ideas outside of the "normal" diet and fitness avenues. I was looking for real change—to truly heal the underlying cause of excess weight. Not just for me, but for all women who struggle with their weight.

During this exploration, I discovered yoga and went on to become a yoga instructor. What I experienced during that training opened my eyes to a whole new world, and I wanted to learn so much more.

I dug in. Over the next seven years, I invested well over $100,000 in trainings, certifications, workshops, and programs to find a permanent and healthy solution to weight loss.

My greatest gift during this journey was finding out who I really am... finding my true self.

Throughout the process, I had to confront many hidden aspects of myself, including the parts of me that I believed were "too much" and unwanted by others.

As a child, my desires and opinions were suppressed.

I asked too many questions. I was too loud.

I was just *too much*.

I felt I wasn't good enough, so I learned to be what others wanted and expected.

Up until this point, I'd been living in a way that was out of alignment with my true self.

And that's why I had been so angry and sad.

No one could see me, not the real me.

I couldn't even see myself.

However, despite not being a religious person, I did believe that there is something greater than us. So, when I came across ThetaHealing®—an energy-healing modality with a spiritual basis—during this time of re-discovering myself, I needed to learn more.

I signed up for a class and soon discovered I had so much to heal. But most importantly, I learned that *it is possible to heal*.

This is when I took a deep dive into learning about the sub-conscious mind and the hidden beliefs that run over 90% of our lives.

As I healed, I realized I could help others do the same.

I was discovering my expertise!

I realized I have so much to offer and embraced my inherent gifts. For example, I found my innate curiosity and ability to ask meaningful questions to be among my superpowers. Connecting with people and asking the right questions comes naturally to me, which makes finding the root cause of people's challenges practically effortless.

I also discovered I am very intuitive, and I learned to trust it.

At the same time, I found my passion to teach others that it *is* possible to heal and change their life! I explored and dabbled in other healing modalities: crystal healing, Reiki, and Silent Counseling. I read books and learned about clean eating, exercise, essential oils, and healthy living.

As my knowledge and experience grew, I finally knew I was ready to start my own healing business, so my clients could benefit from all those years of my personal development. I created Infinite Possibilities in 2016.

At the time, I was primarily helping clients with their self-worth and beliefs about money and success.

Despite the growing pains that came with stepping out of my comfort zone to become an entrepreneur, it was an amazing time in my life.

At this point, the fitness centers had grown to four locations and were running like well-oiled machines.

The freedom of being my own boss was priceless. And I was starting to like myself, to even love myself. It opened doors to a lifestyle I could not have imagined or experienced working for someone else. Prior to becoming an entre-preneur, I had only traveled to Mexico and Jamaica. Since 2017, I have traveled extensively to 14 different countries!

But the truth is, despite the success of the fitness centers, I was struggling with my healing business. It became clear that having passion and running my healing business were two completely different things.

While I was filled with the desire to help others overcome challenges they were going through, I had been learning how to run a healing business the hard way—figuring everything out on my own. I was also working way too many hours and trading my time for money.

It was exhausting.

And not very profitable.

Unlike the franchises.

As I continued teaching and working with clients, I noticed that not everyone got the same results. Some were amaz-ing and life-changing, while others would return to their old habits and patterns. That bothered me, because I believe that everyone deserves healing. So, I continued searching and learning.

That's when I stumbled upon Rapid Transformation Therapy (RTT). THIS was what I had been waiting for!

I signed up for the 12-month training and also became a client. It was surprising to discover the subconscious beliefs I held that created my excess weight. While under hypno-sis, I was gently guided back to scenes that were the root cause and reasons for what was causing my excess weight.

In my first session, I was taken back to being breastfed. Because my mother had five children to take care of, it was the only time I felt really loved and special. So, I had linked food with these emotions. Unknowingly, I would turn to food because it gave me comfort. My subconscious believed it was love.

This was just one of the many beliefs uncovered during hypnotherapy.

After 11 months and a total of four sessions, my body naturally and easily shed 42 pounds of excess fat.

I now weigh 18 pounds less than I've ever weighed in my adult life!

And I did this over the age of 50.

There aren't adequate words to describe what this kind of freedom feels like. I have no desire to eat junk food or sugar, but I'm also free to eat anything I choose; no food is off limits. And I naturally and easily eat small portions, feeling satisfied and content.

But the best part is feeling fabulous and loving my reflection in the mirror.

Combined with everything else I learned, I could now provide amazing results for my clients.

When it comes to excess weight, there are usually multiple hidden beliefs contributing to it. During our sessions, I guide clients into their subconscious memories to *understand for themselves* how and why they got to be this way. I then interrupt the unhealthy looping thought patterns and replace them with healthy beliefs that align with my client's weight goals.

I absolutely love helping women overcome their weight issues because I know that the healing is about so much more than physical appearance. It affects every single area of life—how you feel about yourself shows up in every-thing you do. Not only will it affect your physical health, appearance, mobility, and energy levels, but also your self-esteem, relationships, and how you show up in your business and life.

I help my clients heal from the inside out, so they can start loving themselves again.

When feelings and beliefs are changed at the subconscious level, my clients start to feel and act differently about food, their body, and themselves.

No willpower.

No dieting.

No restrictions.

Sarah, 55, took part in Fabulous YOU, my online group pro-gram for weight loss. Sarah was an Emotional and Addictive eater type. After taking the program, she could see she had been using sugar and processed carbohydrates to disconnect from her feelings.

She was able to identify, understand, and release the old patterns that had her consuming unhealthy foods. She also learned to enjoy food prep, which was a real challenge for her before taking the program.

More than 20 years after swimming competitively at the high school and college level, Sarah returned to her love of water and is now swimming 2000 yards/80 laps on a regular basis.

Sara has shed more than 29 pounds and 27 inches of excess weight. Here's what she had to say about working with me:

"I have released so many unhelpful thoughts and limiting beliefs during my time with Nedra in the Fabulous YOU program. This has made room for a growing sense of self-love! My thoughts, energy, and body are all lighter as a result. This program is amazing, transformative, and life-changing. Highly recommended!!"

Now, just because I had found my passion and begun owning my expertise doesn't mean I didn't face any challenges as I developed my business. Unlike running a franchise, no one gave me a manual with specific instructions and told me what to do.

The biggest mistake I made in growing my healing business was that I wanted to help everyone with everything because I thought I could. In my marketing, I was trying to speak to everyone, but by doing so, I was actually speaking to no one. Those who needed me most couldn't hear me. My message was diluted, unclear, and confusing to them.

The mindset shift I needed to embrace was choosing one area that I was most passionate about and drilling deep into it. Once I did that, I became the expert in that area.

I knew I had something very valuable to offer, but I didn't have a clear message to deliver it. What I've learned is that I *can* help people in many areas of their life, but having one solid expertise-based message makes what you do very clear to your potential clients.

Enter Alina Vincent. With her guidance, I narrowed my expertise, created challenges, and reformatted an existing online program I had offered once, Fabulous YOU.

I learned what I was doing right and all the things I could be doing to make it better!

I had found my expertise, and now, I was learning to leverage it.

As a result of implementing what I learned working with Alina, I had 37 participants and generated close to $14,000 from my reformatted program. I also tripled my rates working with private one-on-one clients.

And while I am *still* learning from my clients, I am also truly moving into owning my expertise now, because I chose to specialize in the area of weight loss.

It's my firm belief that the biggest challenges, struggles, and hurdles we have to overcome in life lead us to our area of expertise. **We are all unique and special; there is no one else in the world quite like you.** Every experience in life matters and has led you to this point in your life!

If you want my best advice around owning your expertise and creating a business around it, it's this: keep growing personally and professionally.

Keep healing and working on yourself.

We can only be as great as our limiting beliefs allow. If you want to shine bright and build a strong healthy business, do the inner work.

You wouldn't know it by meeting me today, but I've overcome so much to get where I am now. I lacked confidence in myself and my abilities; I didn't value myself fully, and I didn't know how to express what I had to offer to others.

To most people, I appeared confident and driven, but

inside, I felt like I wasn't enough, a bit like a fraud.

Who was I to be an expert?

I also feared people finding out the truth… that I'm not that special. That lack of self-worth was actually the underlying motivation behind my drive to succeed.

I was still trying to prove my value.

By doing the inner work, we can transform the way we feel about ourselves and unlearn unhealthy beliefs.

Don't run away from your biggest struggles and challenges. Work with someone like me, who is an expert at healing the root cause of your issue. In the process of healing, you'll find your direction and expertise.

In the experience of overcoming and healing from our difficulties, we find who we truly are, and then, we can use that experience to help others.

Nedra Wendel is a hypnotherapist and the creator of the Fabulous YOU weight-loss program. She has a unique gift for guiding her clients to uncover and heal the underlying issues causing excess weight, so they can easily achieve their ideal

healthy weight and create lasting change from the inside out! After spending 40+ years searching for the solution to her own struggles with weight, she discovered the keys that allowed her to lose 42 pounds and three dress sizes. Nedra now specializes in working with women who are ready to heal their relationship with food, their body, and their self. You can learn more about her here: https://nedrawendel.com/.

Get Nedra's free gift…

The What Type of Eater Are You? quiz to take control of your relationship with food and gain insight into your tendencies and behaviors, here:

OwnYourExpertiseBook.com/gifts

Chapter 6
Overdeliver with Confidence
by Ian Foster

Sometimes, we have to go way back to bring home the "why" behind what we do. After all, there's nothing like personal experience to link us back to a purpose, and the journey back in time to find that "why" is worth it.

You see, I'm a business and tax attorney who specializes in some fairly arcane areas of law. My specialties may seem tedious, mysterious, or puzzling to others. And that's okay. I have my reasons for what I do. It's those reasons that keep me interested in and motivated to help others.

In fact, whatever your area of expertise, there's a good chance it seems tedious, mysterious, or puzzling to me, too. Again, that's totally okay.

We can't all be experts in everything, and each of us must find our "why," so we can own that expertise and use it for the greater good.

My "why" goes back decades.

When I was in high school, my parents were living the so-called "American Dream." They owned a successful manufacturing business with employees who were like family to us. They made a good income, and we lived in a nice neighborhood.

My parents were experts in manufacturing and running a business that provided real value. However, like nearly every small business owner, they were not experts in the ins and outs of tax law. Of course, tax law affected them as it affects all of us—but my parents decided to delegate that responsibility to various trusted advisors.

These trusted advisors recognized that my parents, along with millions of other business owners, were fundamentally ignorant of tax law and feared the government. That's the sort of thing unscrupulous people could take advantage of. So, they advised my parents on how to set up their business and finances in a complex scheme that would drastically lower their tax liability and hide assets from the dreaded government taxing agencies.

"Of course, we promise you it's all totally legal," the advisors in expensive suits assured my parents with impeccable confidence from their corner office with a gorgeous view of downtown San Francisco.

"Look at this fancy legal opinion written by fancy lawyers," the advisors said as they handed my parents a 100-page legal opinion that was so complex and unreadable, "It must be authoritative and definitive, right?"

"I mean, come on," the advisors said. "No high-powered, high-priced lawyers would go to all that trouble and put their reputations on the line if they weren't sure they were correct."

So, my parents bought into the tax-reduction arrangement that looked, to their untrained eyes, totally legit. They "saved" $200,000 in taxes.

As I'm sure you've guessed, this "tax-reduction arrangement" was, in reality, an illegal tax evasion scheme… the sort that ends up hitting you with a hefty bill for back taxes, interest, and massive penalties. If you're unlucky, it's the sort of scheme that gets you thrown in jail.

Thankfully, my parents were lucky. They found a great tax lawyer: someone who gave honest advice and who wasn't afraid to tell his clients what they *needed* to hear rather than what that *wanted* to hear. He explained that my parents were in lots of trouble, and the best thing they could do was come forward, admit their wrongdoing, and cooperate with the government in taking down the criminals who were selling the illegal scheme to unsuspecting business owners.

My parents followed the tax lawyer's advice. They still had to pay back taxes. But the government waived all the massive penalties in return for my parents' cooperation in taking down the masterminds behind the criminal enterprise. Within a year, the government had arrested the people at the top of the scheme and sent them to jail.

That's when I knew I wanted to become an expert in tax law. I was already prepping for law school at that point, and I had a mind for numbers and finance. But it wasn't until I saw how a good tax lawyer made a positive difference in my parents' lives that I realized tax law could be used to help good people doing good work in the world.

I obtained my law degree and went to work for the government, where I spent 18 years investigating violations of business and tax laws. My experience in that position was just as illuminating as watching what my parents went through. You see, I dealt with two basic categories of people: the actual "bad guys"… i.e., people who were cheating deliberately and stealing money from ordinary, hard-working taxpayers, and the many folks who were just like my parents… i.e., regular business owners who lacked knowledge and feared the system, and were thereby ripe targets for scam artists who sold them illegal tax-evasion schemes.

I have seen too many cases of people being taken in by bad advice... beginning with my parents. So, when I left government service and set out on my own, I dedicated myself to helping and serving folks who just want to run a business they love and do the right thing.

Now, I do my part to help people get over their fear of the law and learn enough to stay compliant while saving money.

But I found myself facing a challenge: how could I reach a lot of people and make a wider impact?

Sure, as an attorney, I have one-on-one clients who get the whole range of legal help with business and tax issues. But that only reaches so many people at a time, and there are of course many ordinary business owners who can't afford hourly legal rates. Then there's the fact that most small business owners need knowledge and guidance, not necessarily individual legal services.

That's where meeting Alina Vincent set me on a course to where I am now: *owning up to my expertise in a way that allows me to make a real difference in a lot of people's lives and a good income doing so.*

I first met Alina at her High Profit Programs live event in 2019. I attended it with some skepticism, certainly not convinced that an attorney could run an online program in a way that provided real value to a lot of people. Obviously, Alina convinced me to give it a shot, because here I am, running online group trainings for small business owners who are dealing with myriad business and tax issues.

A big part of breaking through my skepticism was Alina convincing me that I needed to *take real ownership of my expertise*. And that meant several things.

First, owning my expertise means giving myself credit for all the years I've put into developing real-world knowledge in business and tax laws. Many of us who serve for a living are great at telling our clients to be proud of their accomplishments—well, it's okay to be proud of our accomplishments, too!

Next, owning my expertise means recognizing that I really do have something of value to share, and that value extends far beyond my ability to provide individual legal services. I am in a tremendous position to educate and guide people on their own legal journey, so they can get over their legal anxiety and be compliant without fear of government persecution or being taken advantage of by unscrupulous scam artists.

Then there's the hard part: owning my expertise meant getting over my own fear. So many of us are great at helping clients with their fears and anxieties. But getting over our own fears? Ouch.

Well, we need to start taking our own medicine. We need to recognize that *getting out of our comfort zone and stretching ourselves is the path not only to self-improvement, but to making a bigger difference in the world around us*. We need to recognize that it's okay to be afraid; fear is simply our body's natural reaction to the unknown. From there, we must realize that we are safe, and it's okay to try something new.

When I say "we" need to get over our fears, I guess I really mean me, as it's myself I had to convince. As an attorney, I was taught to work and see the world a certain way, and teaching group programs was not part of that training. So, the big unknown for me was whether it was even possible and, if it was, whether anybody would care about or get value from it.

Alina convinced me to take a leap and try it out. And I wouldn't call it a leap of faith. It was more like, *"What do I have to lose by trying?"*

I often tell my clients, "The worst someone can do is say no—in which case, you've not really lost anything." So, I took my own advice, realizing that the worst people could do was say they didn't want my education and guidance on legal issues. If that happened, I'd just keep doing the one-on-one services, which I did enjoy. I also knew it provided value to people who needed it.

So, with Alina's guidance, I created **Legal Protection Made Easy**, an online program for small, service-based business owners. I turned different subjects into weekly modules and Q&A calls. And, lo-and-behold… Alina was right! There is actually a demand for that sort of help!

My online courses have since evolved into regular online monthly workshops that give highly focused and practical guidance on the most important business and tax issues for small business owners. I have a workshop on how to file your business taxes and another on properly forming your business entity. We spend a day discussing client confidentiality and another on the legal issues surrounding social media usage. I then created a workshop on payment and refund policies and another on protecting your intellectual property. You get the idea.

Each training hones in on a specific legal issue or problem and gives attendees practical steps to protect themselves, their business, and their clients, all in a legally compliant manner while saving a ton of money compared to hiring an attorney to do it all for you.

So, yeah, things turned out well for me… all because I *owned my expertise.* I gave myself some credit for all the time and hard work I already put in. I started to examine the real-world value I have to offer to good people who need my help. And I did the hard part; *I pushed through my own fear of the unknown by understanding that I really had nothing to lose by trying.*

I've received a number of testimonials from my clients that leave me feeling humbled and grateful beyond words. But one of them stands out because of what it communicates with so few words …

Lee in California said, "Ian always over delivers! You are safe with Ian!"

I love how Lee's words exemplify what we can accomplish when we own our expertise. When we really own up to how much we have to offer, we can over deliver with gratitude and confidence! We've got nothing to prove to anyone, so we can simply give of ourselves in joyful service. Our clients will recognize that confidence and genuine desire to serve. They'll gravitate to us because of it. Most of all, like Lee says, our clients will feel safe with us… and being able to make your clients feel safe is a priceless commodity. Feeling safe helps our clients push through their own fear and break through their own barriers, so they can achieve the amazing results they so deserve.

Certainly, there are lessons in that journey, both for myself and for those like me who are considering taking a similar path.

For one, it's not only okay to take pride in all we've accomplished... it's a good thing! Once we reach a certain point in life, we've all "been through the meat grinder," so to speak. We've clawed and scratched and sacrificed. We've had the ups and plenty of downs. In other words, our expertise is *hard-won*. So, let's each take a victory lap! We deserve it!

Second, let's look honestly at the value we have to offer. And by *honestly*, I mean take real stock of our extensive experience... our deep and hard-won knowledge and the things we can teach people, so they don't have to struggle in those areas.

Like I said at the beginning, we can't all be experts at everything, so each of us has something to teach the other. Perhaps you are not a tax expert. That's fine, because I am, and I can help! And there are myriad subjects in which I am *not* the expert and need help; that's where you come in!

We are a team on a mission to make a difference, so let's start acting like a team, with each of us playing our role in alignment with the value we have to offer.

Third, there's the fear. We're all familiar with our old friend fear and its cousin, anxiety. It's built deep into our physiology and psychology. I deal with it all the time in the form of my clients' legal anxiety and fear of taxing authorities. A big part of my job is turning down the temperature, helping everyone chill out, and giving my clients tools to heal that legal anxiety and tax fear, so they can take empowered action. And part of all our jobs is realizing that fear is a perfectly normal response to unknown situations; it's not a sign of weakness, but rather an indicator that our minds and bodies are working properly. There's a certain amount of calm resolve and strength to be drawn from that realization, knowing that we're safe and can push our boundaries for the greater good.

All of this is stuff I wish I had known years ago. I'm not saying I have regrets, though. I don't really see regret as all that productive. It's all of my collective life experience that's made me who and what I am today, and I happen to like who and what I am today. I wouldn't be here doing the good work I'm doing and helping the people I'm helping without that experience.

Still, learning these lessons sooner would have sped me along the way, and we can all learn from one another's journey.

I just hope each of us can remember that we have something to offer. We have the hard-won expertise, and we each have our why—our reason for what we do that keeps us motivated and wanting to help others. Again, my "why" goes back to watching my parents endure unnecessary heartache, and then seeing numerous similar suffering as a government attorney. Those people didn't have to be in the spot of having a government attorney like me show up at their businesses with bad news. They were afraid and lacked knowledge (which wasn't their fault!), and unscrupulous tax scam artists took advantage of them.

I chose to put myself in a position that would allow me to impart knowledge and empowerment to thousands of business owners, so they can be legally compliant and save money without fear of scams or prosecution. And that's what gets me excited!

I don't doubt that, when you find your "why," you'll see that it overlaps with and informs your area of expertise. Find that why, and own that expertise. Then, you'll be in a great position to make a difference!

Through his private legal practice and empowering legal workshops, Ian Foster is pioneering the legal specialty of helping heart-centered entrepreneurs serve the world with confidence by being in alignment with the law. Ian passes on his "inside knowledge" from 18 years of experience as a government business and tax attorney, breaking it down into understandable and actionable chunks, so you can build a long-lasting business with confidence and peace of mind. You can learn more about him here: http://www.secondsaturdayworkshops.com/.

Get Ian's free gift…

Ten Questions to Ask an Attorney Before You Hire Them to help you figure out if you've found the right attorney to help you set up your legal foundation properly, here:

OwnYourExpertiseBook.com/gifts

Chapter 7
Harnessing the Power of Mind-Body Connection
by Jennifer Yagos

Even though I was always interested in science and helping people through medicine, I didn't realize that my specialty was going to be in the holistic health field. On the contrary, I was led to believe that I couldn't make money in that field. But life had different plans for me.

In my mid-20s, while going through significant health challenges of my own, I discovered a method that specifically focused on body movement and self-awareness. Decades later, I'm now a body movement specialist, a holistic healing facilitator, and a health coach. I help people harness the power of their mind and body to get out of pain, improve their health, and live a better quality of life. But the road wasn't easy.

While I was in college studying Occupational Therapy and Sports Medicine, I was also dealing with lingering injuries from gymnastics. I sought out chiropractic help and went through athletic training with limited results. I was having constant, nagging pain in my right shoulder and was starting to feel frustrated. At the same time, I was loving everything I was learning about the human body and the brain in my college courses and gaining insight into my own body. I thought I was on the right track to find self-healing and potentially helping other people feel better, too. But the universe was about to direct me toward a journey of learning holistic healing techniques.

Four years into college, I was diagnosed with a brain tumor. What a shock that was! At 22 years old, I was facing the possibility of brain surgery. I was terrified. I was also in denial in terms of doing anything about it; I downplayed the situation. However, in the end, I realized that something had to be done to preserve my health.

Subsequently, I found myself immersed in the conventional medicine realm on a personal level. The surgeon removed the tumor successfully, but throughout this experience, I came to the realization that I didn't want to go into a field that focused so little on the individual. Even though I'm so grateful for what they did to save my brain health, I didn't feel seen or heard. Rather, I felt alone. The doctors were so busy, they didn't have time to fully explain everything to me. And I didn't want to base my career on that model.

Throughout my college courses and internships, I saw how this echoed through the therapy setting, as well. I felt overwhelmed.

It wasn't until a relative introduced me to a movement specialist after my surgery that I discovered a different approach to healing. The method she used eased my pain and improved my body mechanics significantly, enabling me to do whatever I wanted with greater ease and confidence. I was enjoying the individualized attention during my sessions with her and felt that I was being listened to. The constant nagging pain in my shoulder went away. I can definitely say that my quality of life improved.

The private sessions and group classes were so effective that I decided to change my career trajectory, with a new goal of helping people *holistically*.

In 1997, a year and a half after the surgery, I began a four-year certification training to become a movement specialist in the Feldenkrais Method® of somatic education, the modality that had helped me so much.

After many years of nagging shoulder pain along with the lingering effects of the brain surgery resulting from the surgical trauma to my head, I can say that the system I spent four intensive years learning shifted my entire perspective. It eased my pain and other symptoms, and I was feeling so different! I found something that was enjoyable to do, made me feel great, and boosted my confidence in terms of helping myself thrive physically. I became very passionate about this method and was excited to teach it to others.

As a certified Feldenkrais Method practitioner, I discovered that *I became very present*; I could see what was going on with others more clearly, and the experiential process with my own issues helped me see the hopelessness in my clients. And I had the expertise to help them! **My love for this work and its positive impact on my own life inspired me and excited me to help others lead a more comfortable life.**

I started my movement-based business, Motion Freedom, LLC, in 2006. As a movement specialist, I teach people how to make adjustments in their body mechanics to improve health and wellness and mitigate pain. Gaining an understanding of how your body works and finding optimal posture in the process helps you become aware of challenge areas and develop solutions for your body. As the mind and body work together in this fashion, you can improve your quality of life at any age or stage of life!

That's what I love most about the work I do. I look at the entire person, not just an arm, a leg, etc. I aim to change the brain to make long-lasting changes in the body, a process called "neuroplasticity."

I've helped hundreds of people overcome back and neck pain, joint and muscle pain, and migraines. I've helped people mitigate challenges with eyesight, with Parkinson's disease, multiple sclerosis, Ehlers-Danlos (compromised connective tissue), and fibromyalgia. I've helped people navigate challenges with urinary incontinence, sexual dysfunction, and other pelvic-floor issues. I've helped people recover from joint and spine surgery, and I've helped people avoid surgery. I've helped people reduce stress and sleep better.

It's so rewarding to see my clients' quality of life improve. My clients are amazed at how much more fluidly they move from gentle explorations into how their body is meant to function, and how this in turn alleviates pain and allows them to live an active life. My favorite part of my job is seeing a client smile after a session, in wonderment, as they become aware of their transformed posture, reduction in pain, and improved flexibility.

Carla came to me in serious pain after tearing her meniscus at the gym. Seeking to avoid surgery, a friend recommended she work with me. In our first session, I had her lie on her back and guided her through a movement lesson that organized her body in such a way that she was working evenly throughout her body. When she stood up, she felt taller, grounded, and had no pain when walking. That's right—her walking improved from the gentle exercises she was doing while lying on her back.

After just a few sessions with me, Carla was totally pain free. She was amazed. Here is what she had to say: "I've come to learn that the magic of working with Jennifer is using move-

ment to change the brain. She helped me recognize that the body and mind are one. Thank you for restoring pain-free movement!"

Eight years since that first session, Carla has continued to attend my weekly group classes. She found that she was able to avoid surgery because she was pain free and has returned to hiking, yoga, and other activities she loves.

Up to this point, I was really enjoying my career path, helping people reduce and overcome pain, avoid or heal from surgery, reduce headaches, improve vision, relieve back, shoulder, and other joint pain, play with their grandchildren again, travel wherever they wanted without being limited by pain, and continue doing their favorite hobbies.

However, in 2019, I discovered I needed a second brain surgery. Again, I was terrified. But this time, I was determined to do more things to try to heal holistically. I wasn't downplaying the situation as I did the first time.

One of the best things I did was to connect with a neuro-linguistic programming practitioner, and she helped me see myself through a different lens: one of hope, determination, and self-control. I ultimately had to have another surgery, but there was much less fear this time because of the techniques I learned.

Following the surgery, I continued my path of seeking out holistic healing methods, this time with the intention of not getting sick again. This is when I discovered Distance Healing From the Core®, a type of holistic healing that works on an energetic and cellular level to tap into your body's inner wisdom. I wanted to learn more.

Not long after the surgery, I became certified in Distance

Healing From the Core and neurolinguistic programming. I now have the expertise to guide people toward taking control of their health, making wise decisions about their health care, and training their body how to heal on the cellular level… all while being comfortable within their own body from a physical and emotional standpoint.

Now, 28 years after my initial diagnosis with the brain tumor, I have watched myself get healthier and healthier, feeling more and more confident that I have control of my health. My career has progressed into what I have always dreamed about—a spectrum of alternative health offerings to help people live a healthy and happy life.

Since 2006, I worked as a contractor to help people with their health issues. I was working more than 40 hours per week because I wanted to help people so much and had a hard time saying no to someone who needed an appointment. I started to feel burned out and began to realize that I had not been setting healthy boundaries about helping others. This was a recipe for disaster for my health.

Then, along came Alina Vincent in my inbox, and a whole new journey began. I joined her Rising Stars Mastermind, a community of like-minded entrepreneurs who want to make a difference in the world while supporting others who want to do the same. I wanted to share my expertise with as many people as possible, so they could experience the benefits of the powerful skills I had attained.

I had taken a lot of online programs during the COVID-19 lockdown that were already expanding my expertise, and it suddenly made sense that *I should learn how to make my own online program in order to reach a multitude of people who could benefit from my expertise for healing the body, mind, and spirit.*

It has been *so rewarding* to be able to reach out to so many people across the world to teach them how to move better, so they can feel better! After decades of teaching hundreds of people how to restore movement and balance, decrease pain, and return to their favorite activities while managing their mental health and stress levels, packaging my expertise has been such an amazing accomplishment.

I've created an online program that combines the effective healing tools I've learned as an adult with my athletic background as a gymnast, during which time I qualified for state competition six times, placing fifth on the balance beam as a junior in high school.

The five-week program I created is called **Balance in Motion: A Whole Body Approach**. And it sold out! People reported improved balance and confidence, moving more freely, walking without pain, a shift in outlook, less stress, better sleep, and confidence on trails and stairs. One participant stated he felt grounded like a tree with sturdy roots.

What's even more exciting is that since making the decision to create online programs, I've been invited to mentor at upcoming trainings for Distance Healing From the Core and neurolinguistic programming, and I now have time to accept the offers! Finding the business support I needed gave me an opportunity to reflect on my expertise and gave me the confidence to dive deeper into entrepreneurship.

Alina's business and mindset coaching was invaluable. I learned how to hone in on my message in order to convey that I can help make the aging process easier while improving posture, flexibility, and strength at any age. I've owned my expertise, knowing that I've helped hundreds of people alleviate or completely eradicate painful muscles and joints. This happens on multiple levels, through rewiring the brain, speaking to every cell in the body, and educating people through experimental movements on how to find the blocks that are prohibiting their body from thriving and feeling great.

My mindset went from thinking I "might" be able to pull off my vision to getting really excited and clear about pulling it off! I built the confidence to reach out to the world and hone my craft. I'm now combining all three modalities (Feldenkrais Method, Healing From the Core, and neurolinguistic programming) to cater to each of my client's needs. Moving away from mainstream medicine is feeling better and better with every milestone I reach.

As I think back to when I was working more than 40 hours per week, finally reaching burnout, then making the move to shift my focus to an online business so I could reach out to a multitude of people to offer healing support, I feel refreshed and energized. It feels great to have figured out how to share my expertise with more people by creating an online program: a self-paced program people can refer back to over and over again, with the option of seeing me privately online to enhance their learning.

My journey to where I am now was not without bumps, but I now have clarity on my path and confidently shine my expertise out into the world as I focus on helping people live happier and healthier lives. I have released my fear of being able to make a living in the alternative health field. I have been able to embrace the excitement of my new journey. I no longer feel stretched thin.

I had heard about coaching, sure, but it wasn't until I met Alina and joined the Rising Stars Mastermind that I found out how helpful coaching could be in boosting my self-confidence and owning my expertise. If you are an entrepreneur trying to find your path, I highly recommend finding a coach or group of coaches (the group coaching offered in the Rising Stars Mastermind has been absolutely fabulous)!

I only wish I had found Alina sooner.

All that said, if I could leave you with only one piece of advice, it would be this:

As soon as you feel doubts trying to settle in or hear the voice in your head that questions your success, gently replace them with positive affirmations. Hang up words of encouragement in your bedroom, kitchen, office space, etc. For example: "I am aligned with the energy of abundance at all times." Doing this will make it easier to stay in a positive headspace.

You've got this! The best way to prove it is to get out of your own way, take a risk, and focus on shifting your fear into excitement and courage.

If you're passionate about what you do, you owe it to the world to share your expertise by fully owning it and finding and sharing it with your ideal audience.

I'm absolutely passionate about what I do. After helping other people following my own health experiences, I knew I had a gift. That's when I realized my expertise. I knew I could help people, and I knew that I wanted to be more encompassing.

I'm still constantly awed by how much change the body can undergo with subtle, gentle movements. By discovering ways to maximize potentials of the nervous system through postural awareness and self-use, we *can* help unlock new capabilities to regain and/or maintain a healthy brain and body. It's amazing how much our body can do, and I love that I've found a career path that respects the power of the body to heal itself.

Jennifer Yagos is a movement specialist, holistic healing facilitator, and health coach. She helps people tune into their mind-body connection on a deep cellular and energetic level. She has spent several decades honing her expertise to help people live a fulfilling life physically, mentally, and emotionally. She prides herself on treating each person as a unique individual and takes time to really listen to determine the best plan of action for that person's needs. You can learn more about her here: https://motionfreedom.com.

Get Jennifer's free gift…

Your Best Posture, Sitting Up "Straight"

to find comfort and support for your muscles and joints, here:

OwnYourExpertiseBook.com/gifts

Chapter 8
Divinely Guided
by Blanche Boyce

I feel incredibly blessed that I was guided to my current line of work. It's amazing how life can take you on a journey that you never expected or could even dream of, and lead you to somewhere truly wonderful.

I'll never forget the first time I heard the words "qi gong." It was the 1990s, and a friend had invited me to a reiki workshop. There, while working on a young woman who had been paralyzed from the waist down, I heard her whisper "I do my qi gong every day." I had no idea what she meant. I had never heard the words "qi gong" before, but I knew in that moment that I had to do whatever those words meant! It took a couple of years before I was even able to find a qi gong course, but once I did, *I embarked on a journey that changed the direction of my life.*

Qi gong (pronounced "chee gong") is similar to tai chi, only easier to learn. It uses physical movement and postures in conjunction with breath work, imagery, and intention to increase and balance the life force energy (qi) in and around the body. Its overarching benefits include improving health and well-being and increasing longevity. More specifically, it detoxifies the body, strengthens the immune function, improves the senses, increases vitality, calms the mind and spirit, strengthens the organs and organ systems, and reconnects us to our heart and spirit. All this can be achieved in only a few minutes of practice a day.

I loved it from the moment I tried it; I felt so good when I practiced it!

Then, in December of 2000, I was about to leave a Chapters bookstore when a store clerk suddenly pushed a big cart of books right in front of me. I was forced to jump out of the aisle and landed in front of a wall of books. In the moment, I remember thinking that it was like something one might see in a movie; the main character leaps out of the way, randomly reaches out and chooses a book that ultimately changes her life forever. I thought, *"What the hell… I'm going to try that!"*

So, I closed my eyes, chose a book, and randomly selected a page. When I opened my eyes, I discovered that it was about something called "Jin Shin Jyutsu®" (whatever that was) and the page I had chosen was about increasing your lung capacity and improving your breathing by simply holding specific spots on your body. *Huh, what a coincidence*, I thought. At that time, I was doing martial arts training and often had trouble catching my breath! So I bought that book, wrapped it up, put it under the Christmas tree for myself, and then completely forgot about it.

It was a lovely surprise on Christmas morning, and shortly after the holiday hoopla was over, I read it and thoroughly enjoyed it. According to the book, one can simply stimulate a couple of different points on the body to affect it in some beneficial way. I learned that this is a form of bodywork called acupressure therapy. Who knew?? While I had been interested in 'paranormal phenomena' and 'energy work' of sorts in my past, I had never done any body work at all… not even a massage.

About three weeks later, I was picking up my daughter from her job at a used bookstore. She was running a little behind and asked me if I would mind waiting a couple of minutes while she finished the task she was working on. No problem.

As I mindlessly wandered through the aisles, I figured I might as well try that book thing again. So, I closed my eyes and randomly selected one. Lo and behold, it was on exactly the same subject! I figured there couldn't be more than five books in the world written about Jin Shin Jyutsu®, yet two of them had presented themselves to me in quite an unexpected manner. *Was this another coincidence, or synchronicity?* I bought that book, too.

The books piqued my interest so much that I started looking for a course on Jin Shin Jyutsu®. I couldn't find one, but I did see an ad for a training on something called "Jin Shin Do®." I thought they might be similar, so I phoned right away to find out the details. That was on a Tuesday, and the woman who answered said that the last day of registration was Friday. It turned out that taking this course would be tough for me; I had three little kids, and I'd need to drive about 40 minutes each way to get to the 9:00—5:00 classes. It was also short notice, but by Friday, I decided that the coincidence of these two books was too great, and I needed to find a way to take this course.

When I phoned to register, however, I was told it was canceled! I was not only shocked, but in that moment, I knew I was *supposed* to take it. I was suddenly *absolutely certain* that I had been guided to this thing called Jin Shin Do®—so much so that I asked the woman to check again to be sure that it was indeed canceled. She asked me to hold, and when she came back on the line, she confirmed the cancelation but said someone else was going to teach the course in a couple of weeks at a different location. She gave me the details. It turned out that the new course was being offered just a five-minute drive from where I lived, and it was going to be done over a few weekends! I smiled to myself and thanked the universe, knowing how much easier it would be for me to attend. I phoned and registered right away.

I soon discovered that Jin Shin Do® and Jin Shin Jyutsu® are styles of acupressure therapy. Acupressure is like acupuncture without the needles. Finger pressure is used on specific points on the body to stimulate the flow of qi, thereby improving the body in some beneficial way. Like qi gong, these forms of therapy are based on the principles of Chinese medicine.

The course was amazing, and oddly enough, we did a little bit of qi gong before every class. **My universe was aligning, and I was so grateful this work had found me.**

I loved the new learning and began taking all the classes I could find on both acupressure and qi gong. I started doing acupressure sessions with my friends and family. At first, it was just to practice my technique. But I discovered what a rich source of learning doing the actual session work is, and my friends and family discovered how beneficial this form of therapy is.

It wasn't long before I was getting referrals and booking more sessions; the next thing I knew, I had a small business, called Qi Essence Bodywork, doing acupressure therapy!

Around the same time, my friends also became curious about the qi gong I was doing. They started coming over on Saturday mornings for an informal class. I had a lot of fun introducing them to the various forms of qi gong that I had been learning.

That summer, I started teaching a drop-in class at a local park. I collected donations and gave a portion of them to the local women's center, where I volunteered to give acupressure sessions once a month.

When my martial arts instructor heard about my classes, she asked if I would put a qi gong course together for her students. I was up for the challenge!

Qi gong is different from western exercise, which tends to focus on muscle tone. The goal of qi gong is overall health and wellness, and the more you understand the mechanics and underlying principles of what is going on, particularly from the perspective of Chinese medicine, the more you will benefit from the practice.

I developed an eight-week program covering one particular style of qi gong. This gave my martial arts colleagues a look at a softer style of martial arts—one that helps the body heal from the stress of hard style martial arts. I got rave reviews, which led to my developing other stand-alone qi gong courses that I taught at this location. Eventually, I started teaching tai chi there, as well.

I developed a tai chi/qi gong curriculum that I started teaching at a facility closer to home that catered to people over 50. I became enamored with this age group; they cared about their health, and more importantly, about their emotional and spiritual well-being. They recognized the value of the practice not just in the moment, but longer term. They could see how important it is to relax and enjoy the movements. Unlike hard-style martial arts, the goal of qi gong is not to give 110%. Rather, it is to enjoy the ease of movement… to let go of stress and tension in the body and relax the mind.

It was during this time that I realized how all the different aspects of my business came together to support one another. I was able to empower my acupressure clients by teaching them a couple of qi gong movements to support their health between sessions. And unlike a lot of qi gong or tai chi teachers, my acupressure training gave me a wealth of knowledge about what is going on in the body when we do specific movements. I could support a student who was dealing with a health issue, for example, by suggesting certain movements that would help them resolve those issues. My clients and students became more informed, and they loved it!

I also realized how important '**doing the work**' is to learning. I have invested tens of thousands of dollars in dozens of courses, which have given me a wealth of knowledge, but I've noticed that with every session I deliver and each class I teach, my expertise grows exponentially. Doing the practice brings countless benefits that you can't get from just learning the material.

I was very content with my teaching and my session work.

Sadly, that all changed when the pandemic hit. My in-person tai chi and qi gong classes were shut down, and my acupressure clients fizzled.

Now, I *had* wanted to do some online demos and classes, but I was intimidated by being on camera and by the technology I knew would be involved. Fortunately, I was asked by the local women's center to do an online webinar. It was their first online venture, too, and it soon became clear that they knew as little as I did about setting up online classes/webinars! Together, though, we muddled our way through the process, and I discovered that it really wasn't that difficult to teach in the online format. Two weeks later, I launched my weekly online qi gong classes. **The Qi Gong Club**, my weekly online class membership site, was born.

I soon discovered that I loved teaching this way! Without the distractions of a physical classroom, I was able to teach without interruption, and my students were able to focus more intently on the material I was presenting. I recorded the classes, so if anyone missed, they could review the material and do the practice at their own convenience. I was also able to go deeper into the material and cover more aspects of the theory and practice of the movements. Plus, I loved the fact that **people who did not live close by were able to join me and learn this incredible information and method of movement**!

Once I got comfortable teaching my weekly classes, I wondered how I might turn some of the standalone qi gong courses, which I used to teach in person, into online courses. They were different from my weekly classes, where I teach a variety of qi gong styles and various aspects of Chinese medicine, from tai chi to martial arts to acupressure. These courses were more specific, taught over five, six, or eight weeks, during which I would teach one particular style of qi gong. I wanted the courses to be available for anyone to access at any time. But I had no idea how to go about doing it.

That was about the time that the universe delivered Alina Vincent into my life. Once again, I felt guided, and I joined her High Profits Program, a three-day live event on how to create online courses. It was just the information I was looking for! I knew Alina's process would work perfectly for the courses that I wanted to generate.

Putting together my first online course—**Ageless Vitality Qi Gong**—really inspired my creative juices. Although it was on qi gong, I brought in elements from my extensive knowledge of tai chi, acupressure, martial arts, and meditation practice. It was fun to distill the knowledge I had acquired from my 20+ years of practice in these various fields of Chinese medicine.

I had taught the core of the course in-person before, but teaching online is different. For starters, I didn't have to review the material from week to week; if people wanted to, they could simply rewatch the previous lesson on their own time. And I could explain some of the concepts in more detail knowing that people would listen to them again if they needed to. Finally, the slower learners did not hold up the whole class.

I have run the course a couple of times now, and so far, about 40 people have taken it. I have made several thousand dollars from it.

In the meantime, I have created two other qi gong courses, as well.

As a result of these courses, *my audience has tripled, and I am now reaching people all over the world!*

One of the things I love about qi gong (and other aspects of Chinese medicine), is that the benefits are timeless. Whether I offer my courses again next week or in 10 years, the benefits to subscribers will still accrue.

People who I meet online or those who don't live near me are now able to study with me whether through my online courses or my weekly online classes. I even have students who can't attend my live online classes doing my membership program.

Take my student Moya, for example. She took an in-person class with me many years ago. More recently, she approached me in hopes of my helping with some health issues she's dealing with. I met with her one-on-one and designed a specific qi gong protocol for her particular health issues. She also started coming to me for acupressure/medical qi gong session work.

Once her health started to improve, I suggested the weekly online classes as a way to continue her journey to better health. Now that she has returned to work, Moya does the recorded classes, through the Qi Gong Club membership site, when it is convenient for her.

As I have already mentioned, I feel like I was guided to do the work I now do. All of these different facets of Chinese and complementary medicine—acupressure, qi gong, tai chi, martial arts, meditation, and medical qi gong therapy—came together to form my business, Qi Essence Bodywork. But these practices are more than just a business to me; they are a huge part of who I am as an individual. They are woven into the very fabric of my personal life.

Whenever I practice qi gong or tai chi, or even acupressure therapy, I am reminded that the true power of these arts is not in the extensive knowledge I have accumulated about them, but in the practice of doing them—this is where true mastery lies. My journey to mastery is one I have been on since I first learned of these arts, and it's one that I will continue to explore for the rest of my life.

Owning my expertise in these fields has taught me three important lessons that I continue to carry with me. The first is that I am supported. Not just by my friends, family, students, and clients, but also by my higher self and the guides, guardians, and beings of light who surround us all.

I also learned that I am creative! I tend to see myself as more analytical, but when I was putting together my online courses, ideas and new ways of teaching the different concepts and movements would just come to me. I was able to incorporate some of these innovative ideas into my courses, and it made the material easier and more fun for others to learn and remember.

I think my biggest lesson learned has to do with mindset of both myself and others. I have always believed implicitly in the work that I do; I have seen amazing changes in my clients and students. So, when I first started to learn these arts, I wanted to share them with everyone! I've since learned that not everyone is ready for alternative and complementary therapies, and more importantly, it isn't my job to 'sell' them on this work. Those who are interested in exploring new ways of living will usually ask to hear more. Others won't. Either way, there is no judgment; people walk their own paths.

As I reflect on my journey, I truly believe it has been divinely inspired. I had no idea about these ancient arts and their amazing benefits until they were serendipitously presented to me.

If you're unfamiliar with these practices, I invite you to explore them further. It could be the universe's way of giving you a gentle nudge!

Blanche Boyce has a passion for all things related to Chinese medicine. She holds a master's degree in medical qi gong and various degrees in acupressure therapy, martial arts, tai chi, and qi gong movement styles. In her business, Qi Essence Bodywork, she uses and teaches aspects from all of these disciplines to empower her students and clients to fortify their own health, happiness, and longevity. You can learn more about her here: https://www.blancheboyce.com.

Get Blanche's free gift…

Harmony with Motion, a demonstration and document to introduce you to the gentle and graceful art of qi gong movement, here:

OwnYourExpertiseBook.com/gifts

Chapter 9
The Sweet Spot:
Where Your Expertise Meets Your Authenticity
by Jennifer Seidelman

My passion is helping people define, and live, their uniquely personal version of success.

Living in a society that thrives on mass production and conformity, we **don't need more cookie-cutter people or businesses. We need those who have the guts to show up authentically and** share their unique ideas, voices, and gifts with the world.

The greatest gift we can give to ourselves, and others, is the gift of bringing our true selves to every interaction and experience. Authenticity begins with embracing who you truly are at your core and defining what success means for *you*.

I missed out on a lot of opportunities because I was pursuing a version of success that wasn't really mine. That's why I'm so passionate about sharing my story, *so others can evolve into their most authentic selves and live their most authentic lives*… without spending years getting there.

It took me a long time to embrace this lesson.

Now, I'm living a life based on my own individual definition of success.

At the foundation of my success is my coaching, consulting, and training company, Total Success Strategies. I've poured myself into cultivating an environment where people and businesses feel safe to explore as they gain clarity about who they are, what they want, and how to get it. This empowers them to become the most authentic, fear-less version of themselves, so they are catalysts for positive change in our world.

And I *love* what I do!

But I didn't get to this point easily.

I've been self-employed in the real estate industry for more than 20 years, which means I've spent over two decades relying on myself, and my expertise, to make a living. I attribute much of my success in real estate to the fact that I deeply believe personal growth is a critical component to owning a business... if you're not growing, you're dying. Just like in nature, there is no status quo. Things are con-stantly evolving.

Being a real estate broker with a track record of success, I could easily just continue down that path, but *my passion lies in helping others achieve their dreams, goals, and desires.* It's what lights me up! Helping others is what attracted me to real estate in the first place, so I was naturally drawn toward working with others at a deeper level, which led me to becoming a coach.

Throughout my life, and certainly in my real estate career, I've found coaching colleagues came naturally to me. However, when I considered branching out to coach peo-ple in other professions, I believed I had to know *everything* to do so. I was convinced I had to be an expert in someone's industry to coach them. More experienced coaches told me that was not true, but I felt like a fraud when I thought about coaching people in industries in which I didn't have expertise.

Over time, I came to understand that in order to serve my clients, I don't have to be an expert in a particular industry, but I do need to be an expert in coaching and in some aspect of my clients' lives or businesses. It's also crucial that I am continually growing as a coach—ultimately, that's a large part of what my clients pay me for. Becoming an expert at coaching enabled me to serve people regardless of their business, industry, or life circumstance.

In my second year of selling real estate, I hired a "guru" coach. They are prevalent in real estate and have a "one size fits all" approach, which works for some but wasn't what I needed. When I started working with my first "real" (non-guru) business coach, I knew that coaching others was what I wanted to do going forward.

I spent several years coaching only those in the real estate industry.

Then, people in other industries, or those with personal goals, saw the success my clients were having and asked me to coach them too. My client base grew.

By all traditional measures, I was successful. I was doing everything "right": I'd gone to college and grad school, gotten a great job and then an even better one, and launched two successful businesses.

Coming into 2019, I realized I felt very unfulfilled. I was a workaholic, constantly striving for something *more*… trying to find whatever magic combination would make me feel like I'd "made it."

I tried everything: losing weight, moving, ending relationships, working out more, signing more clients. I still felt burned out.

Then, COVID-19 hit.

It became crystal clear to me that **life is too short not to live every day with passion**.

In early 2021, I was having medical issues. My doctors, and those closest to me, were telling me I needed to back off on doing so much and take care of myself.

So, I stepped away from working with my largest corporate client. I knew I couldn't keep pouring that much energy into others, because I wasn't pouring enough into myself.

It was one of the best decisions I've ever made.

That year was amazing!

I reconnected with myself as a human *being* rather than a human *doing*. I gave myself the care, compassion, and support I'd given to others throughout my life. I gained a great deal of clarity on what was important to me, and what I was ready to let go of.

I began considering starting an online program. I had talked about it for years but was scared.

At first, I felt pressure for the program to be for real estate agents. Real estate was the obvious choice when you consider my area of expertise. After all, between my own production and the hundreds of agents and brokers I've coached and trained, I've been involved in thousands of transactions.

I'd just completed the High Profit Programs live event with my mentor, Alina Vincent, and joined her Rising Stars Mastermind. Even she thought I should go after the low-hanging fruit: real estate professionals.

It was the logical choice, so I tried to outline that program. But my heart just wasn't in it.

This was where I experienced a critical mindset shift: *I realized I'd outgrown the version of success I was pursuing.* In fact, I realized that I never actually consciously defined what success meant for me.

I took the time to consider that and realized that the process is exactly what I want to share with others.

I combined my experience and the knowledge I'd gained through decades of reading, training, masterminds, workshops, and coaching in personal growth and business, and in 2021, I developed my **Step Into Success Coaching and Training Program**.

My mission: to help successful people who are questioning why they don't *feel* successful pursue success they're actually aligned with. I help them get through burnout, boredom, imposter syndrome, and that feeling of not being good enough. Then we figure out what being "in the zone" means to them and develop a plan, so they can spend more time there.

It was a success.

Not only did I see the changes in those who participated in the program, I saw changes in myself. The more I worked with my own curriculum and coached others through the exercises, the more I personally stepped into my own vision of success.

Then, in November 2021, I got COVID.

It brought me to my knees. I was very sick for over a month. Then, long COVID set in.

Things went from bad to worse.

I've never dealt with a debilitating illness. I couldn't think. I couldn't focus. I couldn't remember simple words and the names of people I'd known for years. I slept 10–12 hours a night and was still bone tired.

It was terrifying. I didn't recognize myself and felt completely lost.

I had to stop doing pretty much everything in both of my businesses; I simply didn't have the capacity to carry on like I had been.

Fortunately, I had money in the bank and was able to pare down my working hours.

But on a deeper level, I missed the human connections and the growth my work creates. I decided I had to find a way to get back to work.

I took what I learned from Alina in High Profit Programs and applied it to what I was already doing with Step Into Success.

This new version of Step Into Success enables me to *serve more people than ever, and guide them to even better results*—while still maintaining my health.

Although I'm currently back in a building phase, because financially my income hasn't quite recovered from taking all that time off, I'm so grateful that my business gave me the ability to take more than a year away. My business allows me to live my version of success—time and financial freedom—as I make an impact in the lives of more clients than ever.

Working with the clients in my program gives me ongoing reminders that the work I do has a tremendous impact on their health, wealth, career, business, and relationships.

Recently, one of my close friends joined a live version of Step Into Success. I know, "they" say you shouldn't work with your friends, and I was a bit hesitant. She is a licensed clinical social worker, so she's done a lot of self-exploration. I worried my program might be too basic for her.

She showed up, dug in, and did the work. She told me what we did in Step Into Success was different than much of what she did going through school and the subsequent training and therapy she received. Although she hasn't finished all the homework I assigned, she shared that my coaching helped her work through some old "stuff," lay out her goals, and pursue her passion.

Now, she's so clear on what she wants in life that she is checking goals off her list—fast! In fact, she currently has her house for sale (with me, of course), so she can move and pursue a job that aligns better with her new version of success.

Hearing her say that my coaching helped her feels amazing, in part because it proves I truly have expertise in helping people define, and create, their authentic version of success.

In fact, that's one of the biggest mindset shifts I've made on this journey.

If you've spent any time reading articles or books about finding your purpose, you've probably read that sometimes, it can be difficult to figure out your area of expertise because it comes so naturally to you. You may not even realize you're exceptional at it.

That was definitely the case for me.

Before I launched Step Into Success, I thought, "Everyone knows what I know." To me, much of what I teach seems simple. That's because I spend my days immersed in it. It's easy to forget that at one point, everything I now know was new to me.

I started out coaching in the real estate industry because I had experience in it. This helped me feel like more of an expert. And while I soon realized what I have to share spans industries, making that change required a significant mindset shift: believing I had the "right" to coach people outside of the real estate industry.

Personally, I've spent years of coaching and therapy to achieve this mindset shift. I also made a point of learning enough that I felt like I knew what I was doing. As a side note, I've seen some people call themselves "coaches" when they don't have any training or experience. This can actually do unintentional damage to clients. You don't have to be an expert in an industry, but you do need to have the coaching tools and skills to serve your clients.

Throughout the process of becoming a coach, and even now, I remain open to feedback and learning, which ultimately has grown my confidence.

My main piece of advice for breaking through limiting beliefs is to do the work on yourself first.

Sorting out your own issues clears the path for new ways of being. There are lots of ways to do this important self-work: working with a coach or therapist, training, reading, hypnosis, meditation, energy healing, tapping, or any modality that helps you move through whatever is keeping you stuck.

I've learned that part of the beauty of owning your expertise and your personal version of success is that it often heals a lot of blocks you've been carrying around.

And I've found that each time I level up in my business, my personal life levels up, too. My guess is that the same will be true for you!

As with any journey in life, I've learned so much on this path to owning my expertise.

First, your expertise evolves over time, and being "in the zone" and aligned with your version of success requires both knowledge and passion.

Life gives us the opportunity to become experts in more than one area.

Just look at my experience: I felt like an expert in real estate and eventually realized my passion (and expertise) lies in the transformation of people and businesses in many different industries. I began to experience true success once I brought my business to this intersection of knowledge and passion.

Second, there is a space for you in the market. Others may share expertise that's similar to yours, but everyone shares it in a unique way. This was so hard for me to grasp at first. I initially believed that everything I shared had to be new and innovative.

The reality is that the clients who continue working with me do so because of the way I coach. I provide a safe space for them to explore what they want. I ask the right questions, provide feedback to help them find direction, hold them accountable, act as their cheerleader, love on them when they need it, and give them a kick in the butt from time to time… and I do all of this in a way that's unique to me!

The clients who stick around do so because of who I am and how I show up—authentically.

Realizing that is powerful and freeing.

Finally, I've learned that if you want to remain relevant, no matter your field or industry, you must be a lifelong student.

Owning your expertise means you continue to grow… and if you're in business, your clients grow as you do. As a coach, I'll always have a coach of my own, and usually, I have two or three! I see the value in coaching, and therefore, I live it. Part of how I serve my clients is by taking trainings, reading, participating in masterminds, and continuing to learn—not only so I become a better coach, but so I can synthesize what I learn and share it with my clients.

Looking back, my only regret is that I wish I'd jumped in sooner.

I spent so long waiting for permission, wondering if people might see what I was doing and think, "Who does she think she is?" I also spent way too much time worrying about things being "just right."

The truth is, if you're in that mindset, circumstances may never be "just right" for starting a relationship, business, or any new venture.

Along those same lines, you'll probably never feel "done" when you're a business owner. You, your clients, and your products and services will evolve, which is one of the things I love most about being in business. It's never boring! There are always new challenges and new opportunities for growth—ones you may not even be able to conceive of right now.

I also wish I'd trusted myself more. For a while, I listened so intently to the "experts," I forgot to listen to myself. In some cases, I did things a trainer or coach told me to even though they didn't necessarily align with my authentic self or my vision of success. I thought, "I paid them a lot of money, so they must be right."

The bottom line is that *you're* the expert on yourself.

Yes, a coach or trainer can give you tools and training and tell you how to use them. Coaching and training shorten the learning curve and help you avoid pitfalls other people have experienced. You'll go further, faster, with others.

But in order to create success that is meaningful to you, what you do must align with your definition of success. And only you can determine what that looks and feels like.

I do what I do because I believe the world needs more people and businesses showing up authentically. When we do, we make a positive impact on the lives of those around us, whether they're our family, friends, or clients.

The best way to show up authentically—and change the world—is to own your expertise.

I know from experience that it's easier said than done. I also know that doing the work is more than worth it. Stepping into my expertise has given me time and financial freedom, and the amazing ability to change the world!

It can do the same for you.

With a proven record of helping others grow personally and professionally, Jen is passionate and driven to help individuals, and businesses, define what success means to them—rather than accepting someone else's version of success. Then, she draws on her 20+ years of experience in leadership, business, sales, marketing, coaching, and training to partner with clients in reaching their goals. Jen's clients value her knowledge, tenacity, and entrepreneurial spirit, but they grow to love her, dedication, straightforward-yet-kind "tell it like it is" style, infectious laugh, and dynamic, high-energy personality. You can learn more about her here: https://www.TotalSuccessStrategies.com.

Get Jen's free gift…

Your Reality Vs. Your Future Vision video and worksheet to start defining your own personal version of success by getting crystal clear on what is important to you now and in the future—because clarity is power—here:

OwnYourExpertiseBook.com/gifts

Chapter 10
Expertise Equation:
Combining Skills for Success
by Stephanie Newman

Owning my expertise was a skill set I developed over many years of trial and error.

There are five primary facets:

1. Storytelling

2. Modeled Behavior

3. Selecting My Topic of Expertise

4. Learning Technical Skills

5. Failing Forward

Storytelling:

When first learning to read, I loved snuggling with Dad during our nightly bedtime story time. Dad would breathe new life into the story each and every time he read to me. I loved this time with him!

During those nightly story sessions, the seeds to become a great storyteller were planted deeply within me.

Little did I realize at the time that those seeds of storytelling would eventually grow deep roots and contribute to my ability to own my expertise.

How so?

A skillful storyteller holds the attention of everyone listening in the palm of his, or her, hand. There's great power in this!

The way a story is told takes hold of the listener's emotions and guides him/her through unfamiliar territory. The listener simply follows the path presented by the storyteller as the story unfolds.

That's powerful control!

Having fallen in love with storytelling from my early years, I committed to being a great storyteller right then and there.

This storytelling skill set served me well while giving presentations in elementary school, high school, college, and on, throughout a wide variety of jobs over the years.

Yet I didn't quite know how to use storytelling to my advantage while pursuing my dream of one day owning my very own successful online business.

My desire to do so stemmed from watching different families, both friends and relatives, enjoy having control over how they spent their time and income.

I wanted that for myself, too. An hourly job would not provide me control over my work schedule, the ability to create income outside of an hourly wage, own my own home without needing roommates to pay for it, or travel wherever my heart desired.

Until I figured out how to build a successful business of my own, I sought out more experiences that would provide me with answers: new jobs and work settings, and ongoing classes.

Modeled Behavior:

Some people command attention without saying a word.

Patients will allow a doctor to perform a surgery on them after meeting that doctor for just a few moments.

This truth was impressed upon me when I was interviewing an ophthalmologist to surgically place an eye buckle (which is basically a rubber band placed around the eyeball to prevent the eye from changing shape due to increasing nearsightedness) on my right eye.

When I was eight years old, my optometrist recommended that my parents have my eyes examined by a specialist. I was very nearsighted, an inherited condition.

The fragile retinas in each of my eyes were like that from birth. Now that I was being fitted for my first set of corrective lenses, hard contact lenses to slow the progression of nearsightedness, the state of my retinas needed to be monitored through annual exams with an ophthalmologist in San Francisco, California, which was three hours away.

I had these annual eye exams for many years, and each one ended with, "Things look great. See you next year, Stephanie!"

When I was 35, the same ophthalmologist delivered new and unexpected news: "Stephanie, you need a surgical procedure to place an eye buckle around your right eye. It needs to be done today."

Whoa!

Ultimately, the surgeon I trusted since I was eight years old would not be able to perform the surgery due to the medical insurance I had at the time. I was given a list of three surgeons to contact in order of my surgeon's preference.

A couple hours later, I was in Dr. Lit's exam room, and I was shocked!

This guy was YOUNGER than me! And he wants to do WHAT to my eye??

While Dr. Lit buried himself in my case file and mumbled a few things, I truly was not impressed with him.

So, I asked him directly, "Are you any *good* at this procedure?"

Dr. Lit put down my case file, turned toward me, looked me straight in the eyes and said—with the exact calm assurance I needed to hear at that moment—"Yes. I'm *very* good at this procedure."

The way in which he responded to my question was *powerful*.

His body language (looking me directly in the eye) and calm, firm tone of voice INSTANTLY won me over, and I was convinced that I could trust him to perform the surgery. I knew I would have a successful outcome.

WOW! Dr. Lit modeled owning his expertise unlike anyone I'd ever seen before!

That single moment was life-changing. It created an indelible memory of how one day in the future, I would exhibit ownership of *my* expertise to my clients.

I went from doubting this stranger in a white doctor's coat (while wondering if he was even old enough to buy a beer) to complete confidence in his ability to deliver on his promise.

Later, when I built my online business and presented myself to interested people online and in person, I remembered how Dr. Lit convinced me to believe and trust him to get the promised outcome.

I knew if I could convey confidence in what I was saying with my body language, eye contact, tone of voice, word choice, and pace of speech, I could do the same with people interested in my program.

Selecting My Topic of Expertise:

My first topic of choice is to build an online business around: smoothies!

Smoothies meant a lot to me at the time, as they really helped me recover from the eye surgery and realize the benefits of following a plant-based eating style.

After Dr. Lit successfully operated on my right eye, recovery required lying on my left side on the living room couch for three months. I was only allowed to sit up long enough to use the bathroom before I had to return to the couch.

Family and friends kindly dropped off meals and served me. I became increasingly concerned about weight gain and recovery, because many of these meals were "special occasion foods," such as pizza, homemade mac 'n cheese, and casseroles.

I knew I needed to eat fresh produce, but due to the restrictions of movement related to recovery, I was losing hope.

My cousin offered her Vitamix. It was an older model, yet it was nearly brand new and unused. I accepted.

Although my recovery was steady and my sight was pretty

good, I still needed to wear corrective lenses. Eyeglasses were the only option for a year post surgery. For the first time ever, my prescription was the maximum possible. I looked like I was wearing glasses with lenses made out of the bottom of Coca-Cola bottles.

I looked in the mirror and bawled.

I had to figure out how to help my eye recover better.

This moment, coupled with my natural curiosity, led me to a critical discovery and understanding:

If I consumed one green smoothie a day and avoided eating any animal products or junk food, my eyesight improved! It was obvious, by the decreasing need of that strong, corrective lens prescription.

Whoa!

In just three months, the strength of a corrective lens I needed was the same as it was pre-surgery. I was on my way to regaining the level of eyesight that I had before the surgery!

So, I thought, wouldn't it be interesting to see the impact if I STOPPED eating green smoothies? Would my eyesight worsen? Would I need a strong or even the maximum allowed lens correction again?

So, I tried it: I went three months from eating daily green smoothies to three months without.

I still would eat fruit and vegetables, but the trend at the time was to follow a heavy animal protein diet, which I did.

And in three months' time, my eyes *had* worsened, and

once again, I needed the maximum prescription!

WOW!

Eating fruit and vegetables had a direct relationship with the ability of my eyes to heal. And that meant that the outcome was within my control!

When able, I read everything I could find on the connection between health and nutrition. In time, I understood the 'why' behind eating a plant-based diet. Next, I focused on the 'how' to do so in a way that was fun and resulted in scrumptious and satisfying meals!

I grabbed pen and paper and sketched out my idea for my website. Imagine how disheartened I was to discover that my idea had already been done!

Part of me questioned whether owning a successful online business was for me after all. Still, there was a small part of me that absolutely refused to let go of this dream.

The dream would simmer for over 10 years, until I met Alina Vincent. In the meantime, I did what I could to keep hope alive.

Learning Technical Skills:

My initial efforts to bring life to my online business included gaining the technical knowledge of building and ranking websites, starting a YouTube channel, and looking for others doing the same to build a network of people to find answers to common questions related to setting up a business online.

For example, which website builder to use? What are the best methods of accepting payment? How to build website and apply on-page SEO strategies? Which SEO strategies are best for my website's topic? How to drive traffic to my website organically and avoid paying for ads? How to monetize my content and avoid building a gorgeous website that doesn't produce sales? It's commonly understood that the 'money is in the list'… so, how to build a list from zero? And so on.

Plus, life of the online business owner can be isolating, so I wondered how to connect with other like-minded individuals in an environment conducive to sharing information? So many of the folks I met when I was starting out online were secretive about how they built their online business, because they were working from a place a fear: if they shared their practical steps with anyone, it would take away their market share. (Even though the internet was still in its early stages in 2009, so there was PLENTY of space online for everyone.)

I wanted to find people who were willing to share the details of the technical side of building an online business, as well as how to monetize all my efforts. This quest seemed fruitless, yet I continued on it. I mean, I HAD to build a successful online business because that was the only work environment wherein I knew I could excel… because it was far from the usual list of negatives that go hand in hand with a J.O.B.

Truly, I wanted to do only the tasks I enjoyed and hire a virtual assistant for the rest. However, I didn't know where to find one I could trust.

I joined my first mastermind because of the promise to teach me how to build and rank websites. Sadly, they didn't deliver on their promise.

Even sadder, I stayed with them for five years, because I was determined to learn the instruction that was presented in a very hard to understand format. The way they delivered instruction never improved.

In fact, the instructors were more concerned about distancing themselves from the students. After the first year, they were ready to move on to their next million-dollar launch.

I never wanted to join a mastermind again, if that was the common standard.

Failing Forward:

Throughout the years, I took action to build the online business of my dreams. The action wasn't consistent, though, so neither was the forward movement.

I wasted a lot of money on programs and shortcuts that were quick to process payment and negligent in terms of delivering what they promised.

I don't regret these failures, because they helped me see what I wanted in guidance and support to build my online business.

I wanted to join a group where I could receive clear instruction, ask specific questions, get constructive feedback and directions on what to do next, and strengthen my on-camera and presentation skills, all while building relationships with fellow participants for mutual support and feedback.

When I heard from a friend to sign up for Alina's High Profit Programs three-day live event, I also bought the recordings in advance, because I wasn't sure that I'd be able to attend live.

That was the best decision I could have made!

Because I didn't attend the event live. Rather, I listened to the recordings of the event every day while walking around my neighborhood. Soon, I was able to memorize parts of it, because I had listened to the recordings so much!

As soon as I heard Alina share the benefits of joining her Rising Starts Mastermind, I knew immediately that it was where I needed to be, because it would provide exactly what I'd long been looking for:

- Direct contact with Alina each week to ask her questions as I learned to apply her instructions to my specific program idea.

- Constructive feedback.

- A focus on strengthening my on-camera and overall presentation skills.

- The chance to build relationships with fellow students and act as one another's accountability partners.

- Group feedback.

Most importantly, I received the support I needed to work through mindset issues that were keeping me stuck.

I cried a lot of grievous tears the first year as I took steps to build my program. Sometimes, it felt like I was drinking from a fire hose: so much information to learn!

Other times, I received kindness and supportive words to help me move through a difficult moment one step at a time.

Instead of the top concern being processing payments quickly, Alina's mastermind was dedicated to delivering on the promise of providing ample instruction and support via a reliable monthly schedule of Zoom classes and a very interactive Facebook group.

The Rising Stars Mastermind is Alina's way of modeling her teachings. That combination reinforces learning.

I'm so grateful to be part of it!

The best part of joining it is that I was able to realize that I had the skill set upon which to build a successful online business. Rising Stars built upon this foundation:

1. Storytelling
2. Modeled Behavior
3. Selecting My Topic of Expertise
4. Learning Technical Skills
5. Failing Forward

While in Rising Stars, I've been able to create:

- Pilot programs.
- Facebook groups.
- 5-Day Challenges.
- Webinars that convert to sales.
- Landing pages with marketing language.
- Marketing emails.
- Giveaway items and giveaways.
- Video courses.

I've also learned how to:

- Use the specifically relevant technology.
- Build, grow, and manage an email list.

- Set up both marketing and yearly launch-based calendars.
- And more!

I've even ranked in the Top 10 of Alina's Giveaway!

Most importantly, now that I know all that's involved in using programs to build a successful online business, I can apply this learning going forward. I've learned life skills and lasting business-building skills!

How proud I was, earning my first $1,000 through program enrollments!

I'm now in the right place for me, building my online business at the right pace for me.

I wished I'd known all that I've learned from participating in the Rising Stars Mastermind a decade sooner! It's exactly the practical learning I had been looking for.

Living the life of an entrepreneur can be challenging. I'm grateful to have a supportive mastermind group to turn to during challenging times.

Stephanie Newman is an aspiring upscale department store pianist and food whisperer.

As a two-time best-selling author and creator of the Eat More Plants: Mastering the Basics program, she helps clients step out of food confusion and into plant-eating fusion. Through the five simple meal types, clients learn how to quickly and easily add delicious, health-promoting meals into their diet without taking away the foods they love. "All the choice is with you." Doctors were stumped by her medical condition and had no idea where to start. She took matters into her own hands and cured herself simply by eating more plants. For the last 12 years, she has been helping people realize the power of plant-based eating and transforming their health for the better. When she is not hosting VIP days or working with 1-1 coaching clients, you can find her at home practicing her piano for her big Nordstrom debut or out enjoying the beautiful San Francisco Bay. You can learn more about her here: https://eatmoverestthrive.com/.

Get Stephanie's free gift…

101 Ways to Add More Fruit and Vegetables to Your Daily Meals, here:

https://OwnYourExpertiseBook.com/gifts

Chapter 11
Potential Unleashed:
How Helping Others Led Me to My Own Success
by Barbara Lawson

1998 was a very challenging year—not just for the insurance industry, but for me, too. It was a time of radical change as a result of globalization, corporate downsizing, fierce competition, and the creation of lean and mean organizations.

One day, I was called into a meeting and told my services were no longer required. In an instant, my 20-year actuarial career with the company was over. In the blink of an eye, a large part of my world was completely replaced by loss: loss of my income and identity, stability, structure, and community.

I went home.

I took stock.

I was determined to learn how to create the work and the life I love!

Given the unimaginable disruption in the insurance industry and in my life, I concluded having my own business (now Barbara Lawson Coaching Inc.) and being my own boss was the way forward.

To decide what my business might look like, I started by creating an inventory of my expertise, what I was good at and loved to do, dreams I had put aside, where I was unacknowledged, where I had not reached my potential, what my deep values were, and where I wanted to make a difference or contribution to the world.

Looking over my list, I asked myself if I could remember the first time I had owned my expertise.

I found myself reflecting on my childhood.

I have a very vivid memory from when I was just three years old. My sister was one, and my mother said, "Teach her like I teach you, but if she doesn't want to do it, don't make her." Then, she left me with my sister while she did something in the next room. I owned that responsibility from that day forward! I integrated it into my identity.

I *loved* teaching my sister, and later, my brother and any child in the neighborhood. From a very young age, **I learned how to bring out the potential** of children in a way that lets them be their own person, and I use this in my work with my clients to this day.

When I was a little older, my mother asked me to keep a watchful eye on my brother and sister if we were playing outside to make sure they did not do anything dangerous. If they were doing something dangerous and did not listen to me, then I was to tell her. Safety and protection of those who are vulnerable became key values of mine that I have carried throughout my life.

When I did bring an issue about my siblings to my mother, she would assess the situation for herself. She did not undermine my authority, but she taught us lessons. I learned to report the facts objectively and not manipulate my version of the story to get something for myself at the expense of others. **I learned the subtleties of honesty, integrity, and trust when connecting with others and connecting other people with one another**. Our family put a lot of emphasis on building long-term relationships and being able to have mixed feelings and still stay connected… on creating relationships based on trust.

Growing up, my parents taught us to keep an eye on the future. As a family, we took actions long before most people. We viewed school as our first job, and my dad made saving money fun. This taught me **visionary strategic thinking**: keep an eye on the future to keep yourself safe financially.

The next step in taking inventory was to look at my career as an actuary. I had chosen the actuarial profession because it aligned with my love of math and my natural draw to look long into the future and protect individuals.

Actuaries assess risk and project trends in mortality, interest, and expenses far into the future to price insurance and pension products. Also, in my Master of Business Administration studies, I was trained to be CEO of any company in any industry, a key component of which was to see the big picture using trend analysis. This was before the era of people getting single-specialization MBAs. Thus, during my corporate career, I deepened my expertise as a *visionary strategic thinker* with professional training as an actuary and business training as well.

While I enjoyed numbers, during my actuarial career, I was known for my people skills and helping make change within the organization by bringing out people's potential. In fact, I was known as "the graceful implementer." I had transferred my ability to bring out the potential of children to bringing out the potential of adults in the workplace. This, in turn, brought out the potential of the company itself.

When it came to helping people grow, I was not paid for it explicitly. Most of the time, it got in the way of my promotability and the financial reward that I would have received if I had committed to a single actuarial specialty.

Instead, I gained wide experience across many areas of a major international financial services company. From 1980 to 1998, I worked with senior executives on strategic projects that prepared the company to not only survive the period of mergers and acquisitions during the late 1990s and early 2000s, but to thrive.

This experience has been priceless to me when it comes to informing my visionary strategic thinking in a world where specialization is highly encouraged, if not revered. As we move to an online world and a network economy, *we need to see the big picture* in order to come up with solutions to problems that few can easily see, because the majority of those looking at the problems come from a specialist point of view.

I have identified three main areas of my expertise:

- bringing out people's potential.
- connecting with people and connecting people with others.
- visionary strategic thinking.

I made the decision to build my company around my ability to bring out people's potential. I learned of the fledgling coaching profession and knew it would be a perfect fit. I invested several thousand dollars to become a professionally trained coach.

It was June 2000, and I was finally on my way! I was betting on myself and my expertise, and I was excited. My adventure into the unknown began.

And then it hit me:

I had absolutely no idea how to find clients or sell. Serendipitously, in August 2000, my hairdresser told me of an amazing networking group that would be a great fit for me. The following week, I attended my first meeting. I declared to this group of business owners that I was a coach and signed up to join it. I was committed. There was no turning back.

Through networking with the other members, I found business owners and executives to work with right away, and I was able to deliver results.

Take my client, who I will call "Tom."

Tom was VP of Sales at a software company, where he had worked for a year.

The owner wanted to sell the company in three years. To do so, he needed to grow sales from $35 million to $50 million. Tom knew he had what it would take to reach that sales goal within the required timeframe, but he and his boss were in conflict, and Tom was about to quit.

This was a pattern for Tom. In each of the two prior years, he had joined a new company, experienced conflict with his boss, and then quit before moving on to a new company. His wife was beside herself.

Tom hired me.

I listened to Tom describe his expertise.

Then, we worked on three key shifts:

- Tom started to think of his boss like a potential client.

- I gave him an assessment to help him gain insights into his communication style and that of his boss.

- He designed two possible roles for himself.

Six months later, his company announced his promotion. His new role was a combination of elements of the two roles he had crafted. Tom reported his income had gone up by a factor of five.

His wife said to me, "Do you know the peace that you have brought to our home?"

Coaching has ripple effects!

Tom was promoted two additional times and became VP of Global Sales. Under his leadership, sales went from $35 million to the desired $50 million within the three-year timeline. The owner then sold the company, just as he had wanted. At the very last minute, though, to make the deal go through, Tom had to come up with an additional $20 million dollars, which he did.

Tom went on to create his own successful company. I wonder what would have happened if he had not worked with me and just quit the software company instead.

My clients were not only from referrals. I was able to attend networking events and get ideal clients from relationships I developed with people I met.

Along the way, I created my proprietary Vision Alignment System. Using my visionary strategic thinking and methodology like that in the pricing model I used as an actuary, I work with every client to anchor their vision or life-purpose in long-term societal and business trends. I help them identify the skill sets they will require down the road. By taking action to grow these strategic skill sets immediately, they can proactively position their businesses to be ahead of the curve.

In other words, my clients are constantly building upon their skills and deepening their expertise, and that is why they get big results.

Of course, along the way, I had to make some mindset shifts in order to own my expertise.

1. **I had to shift from thinking like an employee to thinking like an entrepreneur.** I had to abandon the comfort of a traditional career path and bet on myself and my expertise. I had to trade knowing for unknowing, and to learn to trust myself. To experience the joy of my visions coming true, I had to experience the risk that they may not. It is this contrast in possible outcomes that creates the sense of fulfillment when a vision comes true.

2. **I had to learn how to talk about my business in a way that would allow people to understand what I do.** Networking and building my business through word-of-mouth referrals was my learning lab. At the core of networking is bringing out the potential of others. My ability to connect with others and to connect people with one another became key. In the same way I listen for my clients' expertise when connecting with them to bring out their potential, I listen for my networking partners' expertise in order to make mutually beneficial referrals.

In the same way that I listen for my clients' needs when coaching them, I listen for others' needs to make referrals to my referral partners, where appropriate.

3. **I had to learn how to get paid for the value I delivered and think in terms of offering packages or programs rather than charging in terms of dollars per hour or on a per session basis.** I found it easier to think in terms of the impact I was making—not only with respect to the primary results a client achieved when working with me, but to the ripple effect of those results on other areas of my client's life, be it finances, health and wellness, relationships, or potential.

These mindset shifts had lasting positive effects on my business. For 13 years, I brought in consistent income every single month. I was living the life I loved and helping others do the same! I was very grateful.

The next major disturbance to my generating consistent coaching income was taking on the care of my elderly parents. I would not trade a minute of the extra time I got to be with them; however, it did affect my business and my availability to network for the following six years.

Then, just as I got back into networking and rebuilding my business, along came the COVID-19 pandemic. It was difficult to get clients, and my income was limited by the number of one-on-one clients I could coach in a month. I decided that the time was right to move my business online, so I could reach more people.

Within six months, I heard of Alina Vincent and her ability to help business owners package and monetize their expertise into an online program. Alina's process allowed me to create and deliver an online program in five weeks—it was the fastest and most effective system I have seen. Using it, I was able to package my ideas and quickly test them out in the marketplace.

I chose to create my **Money Mindset Makeover** program, which focuses on helping business owners make and keep more money.

Getting my pilot program off the ground was a lot easier than I expected. So was filling it, which I did by simply reaching out to business owners in my network. Six people signed up at $197 each for a total of $1,182.

And program participants gave me great feedback.

One of my participants, a travel advisor who is gifted at creating memorable and exciting travel experiences for her clients, said:

"A simple mindset shift about owning the value I deliver has enabled me to effortlessly charge for a customized service that I used to provide for free, resulting in a significant and welcome contribution to my bottom line after surviving the devastating effects of COVID on the travel industry." - Dawn Cove - Travel Advisor

Another of my participants, who is also one of my referral partners, said:

"Barbara is a wealth of knowledge and insight. She is always thinking five steps ahead. She uses her beautiful mind to plan, strategize, and create business opportunities for her clients and her referral partners. I'm happy to refer her as a coach and strategist because I know, from experience, she pulls great ideas out of me and shows me ways to monetize them. She

can do this for you, too. With Barbara's assistance, the sky's the limit."- Leo Johnson, House Painter, Artist

As sometimes happens after first running an online program, I realized its scope was too broad and too deep to be run as a five-week program. I gained the clarity that it was not the first step on a client's journey with me; rather, *it was the foundation* of my group coaching program/mastermind.

So, the question was: what problem should I be helping my clients solve before they work on their money mindset?

The answer was not easy for me to see. However, Alina is passionate about helping business owners recognize their expertise, and she started to shine a spotlight on my knowledge and experience building my own business through networking and word-of-mouth-referrals.

This led me to the idea of creating a new five-week program, this time to help business owners who want to consciously get clients from connections they already have.

I decided to take on a couple of one-on-one private coaching clients to test the material first and create the program outline from this research and development perspective.

People sometimes ask me for advice when it comes to owning their expertise before starting an expertise-based online business. Here is what I tell them:

1. **It is very important to have mentors to guide and support you**, to reflect to you who you really are and shine the spotlight on your expertise. Sometimes, your expertise is something you cannot see for yourself. Other times, you can see it, but you do not know how to

message, package, or monetize it.

2. **Join a small community of supportive associates** with whom you can talk about your business or professional plans, so you will have a foundation of support and a stronger network when expanding or needing something.

3. **This is a lifelong journey.** In order to stay passionate about what we do, remain fulfilled, and continuously make money, we need to continue to grow and to deepen our expertise. I will review my expertise every year, to see it in a different light. We have often done things before that can inform or lend credibility to what we are currently doing and even repurpose something we have done in the past to generate more income.

I have learned and grown so much since taking the risk to create my own coaching business focused around my core expertise of bringing out the potential of people, their jobs, and their companies.

I hope after reading my story, you will feel inspired to explore your own expertise and create your expertise-based business and the life you truly want to live, too.

Before starting her coaching business in 2000, Barbara L. Lawson, FSA, FCIA, MBA, worked for international corporations in the financial services, telecommunication, and food industries. Her passion for helping people realize their full potential and her desire to build a business that supports family life inspired her to become a coach. Barbara has combined her years of experience as an actuary, business strategist, and coach to help business owners make more money in these uncertain times and create the life they truly want to live. Barbara is a Fellow of the Society of Actuaries and of the Canadian Institute of Actuaries, an MBA graduate of The Ivey School of Business (University of Western Ontario), CoachU and Coachville. She lives with her family in Toronto, Canada. You can learn more about her here: https://www.barbaralawsoncoaching.com.

Get Barbara's free gift…

The Money Profile Quiz to discover which of the seven Money Profile styles is your key to monetizing your expertise doing something you love, here:

https://OwnYourExpertiseBook.com/gifts

Chapter 12
Joining Hands and Hearts Through Healing
by Linda S DeNike

As soon as the world shut down due to the COVID-19 pandemic, the obvious solution was to offer my classes on Zoom. In order for me to succeed in this online arena, however, I soon found out that I really had to dig deep and figure out what made me unique and how to describe it to others, so they could find me. I needed to take ownership of my expertise.

Before the pandemic, I was working under the umbrella of the local Senior Center teaching back-strengthening classes, training dancers, and teaching choreography to my dance group.

But let's go back even further, for a moment.

I first read the book *Summerhill: A Radical Approach to Child Rearing* while in high school. It describes a style of learning according to your interests. In other words, you could read, write, and learn math, science, history, and social studies based upon your unique interests. I wanted this approach to learning!

You see, at age 10, I started taking classical ballet classes three times a week. And I loved it!

My dedication to, and love of, ballet grew as I entered junior high and began taking daily classes. In high school, I took multiple classes per day. Additionally, there were regular company rehearsals, for which I would understudy.

It was in these classes that I began to notice that I was in sheer, heart-flung-open love when I danced. I remember a beautiful company dancer telling me during one of her rehearsals to make sure I continue dancing, because I had something special. It was such an honor to be acknowledged!

I want to interject that it was in assisting in the young children's classes that I became a ballet technique geek. I loved drilling the basics and becoming strong in them. It came in handy when trying to understand how movement is formed by our muscles. It still pays off big time now, too, because these ballet basics and other strength and alignment-supporting exercises are exactly what I use in my Sage-Age Women's Movement classes to rebuild aged bodies.

I was very interested in Russian ballet, and one of my ballet teacher friends had been to Russia several times. She began to school me on the steps to take in order to embark on such an adventure. She had befriended Kirov company dancers and was invited to take company classes as a guest. This sounded great to me.

Thanks to reading *Summerhill,* I knew that the only way for me to learn was through my interests. When I did that, I became not only skilled in the topic, but passionate about it. I then naturally taught others what I learned.

So, I brought this idea to my counselor and asked if we could craft an independent study program for me—one that would allow me to learn language, history, music, arts, math, and geography around my main passion and interest… dance.

His response was, "No can do, so sorry." Shot down and let

down, I gave up on school. I just couldn't wait to get out at the end of the day and get to ballet.

At age 17, I left home to join an approximately 100-member dance company with its own orchestra. This company performed dances and music from the Balkans and Central Asia. I also learned about choreography, staging, working within a group, developing stage presence, and the art of quick changes.

I was introduced to beautiful cultures rich in tradition, music, dance, national and regional dress/costuming, language, and a bit of geography. While a bit of my dream was being fulfilled at this point, I must say that my greatest interest was in styles of movement within dance.

However, this company didn't offer the technical and rigorous training I was used to, so I also trained in competitive Highland Dance. Doing so added another layer to my dance bag of tricks. I didn't really enjoy competition, though I did quite well, taking home first-place trophies and plaques when I competed.

Though the big company was year-round, I performed in side gigs, as well. I would dance yearly six-week runs at the Northern and Southern Renaissance Pleasure Faire. Originally, I was hired as a dancer for the Scottish show to perform the typical Scottish Highlands and National dances. As it grew, it was paired with the Celtic Parade. Having befriended the Irish step dancers, we invited them to join us in our shows. Being groomed in choreography, it was a natural step to take the old standard dances and expound upon them, making them into choreographies. This came easy to me, as my mind saw things in shapes and patterns that would flow one to another.

I would recruit dancers from the big company, train them in the style of Scottish dance, and teach them the dances. They would then join me for a weekend of dance performance at the Faire. I loved dancing with my stage-trained, audience-friendly, dance-performance friends.

So, from single dancer and piper on a small stage to main stage shows that attracted huge crowds, so evolved the Celtic Show with Scottish Dancers.

Having already trained the dancers from the big company, I was able to share this form of dance with the big company. It was in this manner that me and my dance colleague choreographed the Scottish Suite for the big company. This was a high time with me doing what I did best: dancing, training others, choreographing, and performing.

Because of my history with the Renaissance fairs, the entertainment director asked me if I would choreograph a Cancan for The Dickens Christmas Fair held from Thanksgiving to Christmas.

Absolutely, no problem! How fun!

I worked with the orchestra director to arrange the music from Gaite Parisienne. I listened to the music repeatedly, pulling the parts that caused images of movement and the story to evolve in my mind. I recruited dancers from my ballet training days and from the local dance school… even one of the Irish step dancers. We would meet, collaborate, and create. My boyfriend and I designed custom costumes for the eight dancers, and we created a crowd-pleasing Cancan.

At a later date, the opportunity to resurrect the Cancan with the big company dancers presented itself. Again, I worked with the orchestra director to teach him the arrangement and five fast-learning women dancers, teaching and adapting the choreography to their abilities. All set and ready to go, we performed for the benefit held at Diane Disney's estate. I was also able to perform a Scottish duet with my dance partner of many years. Taking an old dance number and choreographing the stage movement on the fly, I whispered the next moves as we performed, big smiles on our faces. Just writing about this gives me as much joy as it did then… maybe more.

Over a twelve-year period, I performed in various dance companies and dance troupes.

At around age 27, I had a major experience that I later realized was a spiritual awakening of my sixth chakra. It was as if my forehead exuded a beam of light as I experienced a magnetic pull toward a mysterious unknown. I couldn't focus on anything else in my life, not even dance. So, I left my dance life and returned home to the San Francisco Bay Area.

I began to find answers when I entered into the world of psychic energy. First, I sought out clairvoyant readings and healings, and then, healing and meditation classes.

The school's focus was on becoming confident in your own clairvoyant sight and your spiritual nature. I set my sights on the Clairvoyant Training Program, and once I joined, I was reading and healing almost every day after work on weekdays.

The duration of the training was just shy of two years, and at that time, I had to make the big decision: whether or not to join the staff and take the teacher's training program.

I would also have to be ordained as a psychic minister. I struggled with claiming to be a psychic, let alone taking on the title of "minister." But because I loved energy work and was good at it, I joined a volunteer staff of dedicated ministers and became known as Reverend Linda. I taught beginning classes from the prescribed outline and continued to read and heal while getting paid a percentage of the earnings from my classes and readings.

About seven years into my training, I experienced a profound turning point while in session with my teacher. The result was my clairvoyance opened up even further, and my reading skills became very accurate. It later became referenced as "The Light." This experience taught me about being aware of my spiritual nature and the high-frequency energy of love. It moved me from dedication to my energy work to dedication to learning more about divine love and my soul nature through my energy work.

I was really good at focusing and practicing my psychic skills. My teacher told me that I was very diligent in the manner in which I did the techniques, and that this was not the case with everyone. I was very surprised to hear that.

From there, they gave me the advanced level clairvoyant training program to teach. In order to enhance the students' reading skills, I was to train them in the manner in which I did these techniques. Wow, humbling!

In talking to one of my students from that time, she told me that she vividly remembers the methods I taught her and how I encouraged her to practice. She shared how much she enjoyed my precise style of teaching. She is now a clairvoyant reader and instructor in intuitive studies. I was so honored to hear that I was a part of her being able to help other people!

I really cherish my psychic and spiritual training, and I have shared some of my most profound highlights with you. In working with people today, they are always present with me and part of me. They are the reason I continue to work with others.

Unfortunately, the school's emphasis moved away from doing what I loved to keeping the school and foundation operating. The long hours weakened my body, my constitution, and my self-esteem. After 20-plus years, it was time to move on and take all that I learned to heal myself and rebuild a healthy relationship with my body.

Then came the time when I desired to build physical strength again, so I went to the local senior center to try out some of the classes they offered. To my surprise and great pleasure, the director, a gracious Russian woman, recognized me as a dancer. After a long conversation about my dance background and love of Russian ballet, she asked me if I would like to teach at the center.

I was honored to be recognized for my talent.

And yes, I would love to teach again!

They had recently lost their folk-dance teacher, so I started there. Then, I offered a warm-up class before it. I was given free rein to teach what I wanted the way I wanted. This was a license to go into my creative mind and really draw on movement that would benefit everyday life. I wanted to provide classes that would help regain postural alignment and freedom of movement from foot to head. I wanted to help people suspend the story of what they can't do anymore and help them regain some of what they could. I eventually evolved the warm-up class into a back- strengthening class. They were inspired, and so was I. I would often hear the students explain how they came in the door in pain and left without it. They shared other amazing and unexpected achievements that they attributed to what they learned in my class.

I was not only strengthening my body, but helping a whole group of people do the same.

And, in honor of my love for dance, the folk-dance class evolved into a dance performance troupe called the Lovely Ladies Dance for Health that would perform for the senior community and occasional fundraisers for the arts.

Life was hunky dory!

And then… the shutdown.

Within two weeks, I transferred my in-person back classes and dance training to online, teaching on Zoom. And I began the search to learn how to get found in the online world.

That is when I found Alina Vincent.

I signed up for Alina's Visibility Kickstarter Online Challenge. I was impressed by how she presented the information in easy-to-understand, bite-sized pieces. That led me to her High Profit Programs live event that was all about creating an online program. Perfect!

I always liked the idea of generating residual income, and this was a great way to do it. Then came the possibility of being mentored in Alina's Rising Star Mastermind group, and I really felt like it was an aligned opportunity for me. *And* she had a healer on her staff. Super fantastic!

I am now in my second year of the Stars and have created four programs to date: Give Yourself a Raise, How to Stop Overthinking & Take Action, Effortless Manifestation, and Back Pain Relief. With them, I toggle between practical energy work programs and body-mind fitness.

And I've seen the financial results of creating online programs, as well. For example, my latest, **Effortless Manifestation**, had seven participants at $98 and yielded $686. My private session, Holistic Body coaching, has yielded $2,250, and my Empowered Heart Sessions $2,285.

Most importantly, I can see how the work I do helps my clients, as in the case of Miss Muriel:

Nine years ago, Muriel came to me at the age of 81. She had bad knees and walked with a cane. For five of those years, she performed in the Lovely Ladies Dance Troupe. We've seen her through breast cancer, an undiagnosed heart condition, and recently, COVID. Yet I can hardly remember her ever missing a session.

Recently, Muriel said, "My heart would not be doing this well if you weren't my mentor." She has really embraced what it is to listen to her body and center and recover her energy when it is required without self-condemnation or thinking less of herself.

She is currently venturing into deeper studies on energy healing. When she heard about my new monthly healing circles, she was delighted with the idea of "having something to do" … a deeper purpose at her awesome sage-age of 90!

Now, having combined my over 40 years of experience and teaching others in psychic/soul energy work and spiritual studies with my background in dance performance, I've brought my medley of talents together to form my very own business, Holistic Mind & Movement.

There are several things I've learned along the way in terms of owning my expertise and building my business.

The first thing I had to do was realize that *having a passion and a talent for something is not the same as owning it as your expertise*. For me, it was easy with dance, because I absolutely embrace it with my whole heart. I can truly say that what I do with dance and movement and how it helps others is my expertise.

At first, though, I could not say the same for energy work, healing, and clairvoyant readings, even though I had years of experience in it and was skilled at it and loved it. I had to do some energy release and healing in order to embrace it, align with it, and fully own it as my expertise. I am proud to say that this year, I have added energy healing back into my offerings.

I have also discovered that the more I own my expertise, the clearer the mission of my business becomes: to help others heal, especially their wounded hearts. **I am on a mission to help sage-age individuals get their bodies up and running and join hands and hearts through healing.**

The more I own my expertise, the easier it is to talk about it. The experiences of past clients and students—what they came to me with and what I helped them with—as well as my own personal experiences, gives me the information I need to appeal to the needs of my aligned clients.

If someone asked me what advice I could give them to help them own their expertise, I would have to speak from my own experience.:

My biggest takeaway from my life experience and owning my expertise is that you have to raise your vibration. The energy we encounter in everyday life, as well as the energy stored within us that presents itself as blocks, is heavy. It keeps us down, clouds our perception, and definitely affects how we feel about and perceive ourselves. There is nothing light about it. Most of all, it is not our authentic energy as spiritual beings.

I realized the more I raised my energy, the clearer I became. I could easily connect with heart and soul and clear the clouds of despair that obscured the things I love, was passionate about, and skilled in. Then, I could own my expertise wholeheartedly.

In my mind, that is what we're here to do: refine our person to the point of delivering ourselves through all that we do.

Linda S DeNike works with sage-age individuals who have big things to do in their life in a fit body to boot. She has 40 years of dance and healing movement experience and well over 20,000 hours instructing sensitive souls in healing and intuitive energy studies. She brings it all together in her business,

Holistic Mind & Movement! You can learn more about her here: https://LindaDeNike.com.

Get Linda's free gift…

A guided meditation to Give Yourself a Raise, here:

https://OwnYourExpertiseBook.com/gifts

Chapter 13
Overcoming Inner Obstacles:
Unlock your Potential
by Aparna Vemuri

Perceiving that you possess expertise that can aid others is not the same as owning your expertise.

I can tell you from firsthand experience that realizing your skills can be exciting. However, in my case, self-doubt crept in around whether I could help others using my newly found expertise. That delayed the process of fully owning my abilities.

In fact, becoming a healer who casts her magic on others was a long and difficult journey!

My mother, who studied until fifth grade, always wanted to see me become a doctor. Back then, I really didn't know what I wanted to do or become. I grew up like any other normal, funny, witty, and carefree girl. But eventually, I failed her dreams by becoming a dietitian.

My father expired when I was 14 years old, and that brought a halt to my carefree style of living. I experienced some paranormal experiences, but they were denied by people around me. So, I started shutting down as the fear of rejection and ridicule kept me from sharing my experiences.

In 1995, I got married to my maternal cousin. I always dreamt of having a big family, living together with extended family while my in-laws pampered me. Rather, I had to learn to live in a nuclear family.

Life moved forward with no complaints whatsoever. There

were no triggers because I was blessed with a loving husband. However, I felt an emptiness deep within. I didn't know what it was or how it could be filled. Then, I had my first child—a blessing in disguise. He came as my best teacher ever, and I was totally enjoying his presence. At the same time, his actions as a three-year-old caused certain kinds of emotions to surface in me.

My son is a very lively and active kid. My husband and I have to remain vigilant to ensure his mischievous behavior doesn't bring him any harm. At the same time, observing his attributes and behaviors made me think about my own childhood. I used to be that active and energetic girl, too! I was a free spirit and could do as I pleased.

Now, I was realizing I had changed. I was not who I once was. I lost that liveliness. I had been attempting to live up to the expectations of people around me so much, I wasn't aligning with my true self. This led me to feeling constrained and unable to express my natural gifts and abilities.

That's when I had my first encounter with energy medicine. A Reiki teacher appeared in my life and taught me both first- and second-level Reiki. After completing the Level 1 training, which is mainly focused on healing the physical body, I questioned whether I had received the training properly. I did the same with Level 2. However, internally, I realized something was shifting at an emotional level. I could feel and sense my feelings.

This was a period of joyful and sad moments fighting with each other to dominate my psyche. I was working as a dietician. This is the only instance where I felt that I have been able to apply my expertise in nutrition to serve others. One day, I had an opportunity to help my husband, who was living far away and from India, with a job interview. In that moment, I knew I had to embrace my abilities, set aside all my doubts, and help him be confident facing the interview. I did a Reiki healing session with him for 15 min.

Behold! I felt a surge of energy in my hands. I felt my heart expanding and a complete moment of being in a space I had never experienced before. I had something magical in my hands, and I knew I could share that magic with others! That's when I decided I absolutely had to become a full-time healer.

My journey toward doing so started just like any other healer's… with self-healing and self-awareness. Before my first remote healing, I was not fully aware how I could help others. I started with my relatives, friends, and their friends. I really enjoyed doing that healing, because I was not only helping others, but also expanding my awareness of the Universe. I was meeting more and more spiritual teachers and ascended masters, as well.

However, over a period of time, I started feeling very frustrated and irritated, which began affecting my family. I had been so excited to define my own time and hours of work as a healer. Yet there I was, frustrated, because I wasn't assigning any value to the transformation I bring to people. I was also irritated because people were taking advantage of me and my time by calling in last-minute cancelations and demanding new appointments. Yet I was not able to say no.

That wasn't even the biggest lesson I was learning!

When my mentor asked me, "Are you charging for your services?" I admitted that I was not. She said, "There's a lot of imbalance in giving and receiving. That's impacting your emotional health."

And *that's* the biggest lesson I ever learned. People always talked about how healers shouldn't charge, when they are simply deriving the energy from the Divine. It's Divine work, and how could anyone charge for that? This is a kind of paradigm society forces upon healers.

So, in order to bring back balance to my giving and receiving energies, I started charging for the quality time I spent with my clients. I also loved watching my clients benefit from our work together!

In early 2009, one of my clients, Ms. R, said, *"You have guided me beyond any of my therapy sessions to heal and helped me to overcome my past traumatic abusive relationship experiences."*

And that made me realize that, even more than healing, **I had been coaching and guiding people to take action**.

Which made me think… how would it be if I could reach and help even more people?

In 2010, I started conducting group sessions. I not only provided guidance and healing, but also invited active participation via specific actions to better participants' lives.

In 2012, through a telesummit, I was fortunate enough to have 98 people sign up for my program! This made me realize how important it is for me to amplify my voice to guide people and help them connect with their inner spark.

However, after the initial surge of dopamine, I felt the fear of rejection rear up again, which led to fear of failure deep inside of me. These fears walled me into a prison of self-doubt, and I was stuck there.

I also recognized internal conflict around my priorities and responsibilities. I felt like I was hiding behind my responsibilities so as to avoid all my fears!

I wasn't accepting opportunities to be on bigger platforms. I confined myself to the clientele I had. However, this made me restless; I had ultimately restricted myself. So, in order to bail myself out of my own self-crafted mental prison, I started working on personal growth with the help of books and mentors.

I explored the "WHY," which is very mystical. It can be the root of all suffering and/or the cause of awakening. It accomplishes the latter by making one realize that you need help out of your emotional wound.

I learned that I needed to heal the wounds that were causing the fears. One was created when I was in ninth grade during music class. My teacher asked anyone who wanted to come to the stage and sing a song of their liking. My older sister was also in the same class, and I started singing a song that we both loved. After getting through only the first line, the teacher asked me to sit down. That's when I felt rejection, which became a fear of rejection wound.

Healing wounds is a journey. It's the peeling of onion layers. You peel one layer and have a period of integration. Then, another layer shows up, and you peel it, and so on. The Universe is perfectly orchestrated to bring to our awareness what needs to be addressed when we are on a personal growth journey!

As I began to embrace my calling, things began to fall into place for me. In 2017, I saw the vision I'd committed to

15 years before come to fruition—I started my business, PersonalTransformationPathways. Through it, I was teaching, coaching, and healing in my group calls.

In 2019, I became a Canfield Certified Trainer. This helped me come out of my shell, as it required me to share and be on stage in front of other trainers and three mentors.

Starting from that point, I had the opportunity to work with different mentors who supported my personal and professional growth. And I was truly enjoying my success!

However, my path took an unexpected turn when I attended Alina Vincent's High Profit Programs live event in 2020 and subsequently joined her Rising Stars Mastermind program.

Working with Alina helped me to enhance my existing online programs to make the content concise. Her support made me realize things can be much easier than anticipated with the right mentorship. Her teaching helped me focus on my work and marketing and expand my business. Her guidance gave me more clarity and the nudge that I needed to put all my thoughts and experiences together to support more people on their journey.

Not only that, but the group members support one another to be the best version of themselves! One person from the mastermind challenged me to do a Facebook live. I accepted and started doing live videos on my Personal Transformation Pathways page. My number of followers increased from 15 to 695! This helped me to trust myself more than anything else.

Now, when it came to structuring my online program, I admit I initially struggled to understand how to create a healing online program in pre-recorded videos. I shared with Alina how my clients enjoyed my live calls with healings, clearings, and activations, and that I, too, enjoyed interacting with them and seeing their transformation occurring right in front of my eyes. Alina suggested I have a live session every week, and boom!

I followed her formula to create a structure—an online program—that can function for years to come, which means more people can benefit from it. I created $8K when I first offered **Divine Matrix Your Path to Abundance Mastery**. (After that, I implemented her input into my various offerings with great success!)

My participants experienced success, too, as the program guided them through uncovering the blocks that needed to be addressed first, which would in turn open them to receiving more abundance. Here's what one had to say:

"I took the course to enhance my career, but I noticed that my health improved, Finances automatically improved as my career enhanced. I got around 10 clients who are taking regular sessions with me, and they are referring me to more people. Throughout the five-week program, I worked on overcoming my limiting beliefs and gained a newfound understanding of my emotions. As and when I become aware, I use Aparna's holographic tools to remove them. It's so simple, yet powerful."

Spirituality is often perceived as a separate aspect of our lives. However, the truth is, we are all spiritual beings, and spirituality is an inherent part of who we are. That's why all my programs include food for spirit, as well, as shared by this participant:

"Aparna Vemuri is a great inspiration in bringing psychological and spiritual dimensions together and helping us clear our internal blockages. Her practice worksheets are great and grounded; that surfaces the right blockages and helps us realize the need to either clear the blockages or part from our way. Her worksheets and tools are well-designed and foster empowerment. You can practice everything as a daily routine even after the course. Her clearances are very powerful and impactful, and they facilitate a better vision to uplift our spiritual esteem. Her scenario-based clearances followed by deep-rooted spiritual guidance helped me keep balanced and grounded during chaos."

Speaking of Abundance Mastery… I'd love to give you a taste of the type of coaching I do!

As you know, our society places high importance on money. Consequently, we tend to associate abundance with financial prosperity. However, to draw wealth toward ourselves, **we must cultivate an Abundance Money Mindset**.

There are five key elements that play a vital role in attracting money. If you currently feel content and financially secure, then you are on the right track. However, if you are not, it's beneficial to examine what is missing and blocking your financial flow.

Exercise: 5 Powerful Questions to Increase Your Money-Attracting Factor

Step 1: With a journal and pen, find a comfortable, quiet place.

Step 2: Close your eyes and take a few deep breaths.

Step 3: Slowly open your eyes and go through each

question below. Spend a few minutes on each one and write what is true to you. Remember, only YOU know your answers. Nobody is going to judge you. So, answer them honestly.

Question 1: Joyful: Being joyful unlocks more opportunities and money. When you take a look at your life, do you tend to experience more joy, or do negative emotions dominate your life?

If negative emotions dominate your life, think about what makes you joyful. Write them down.

Question 2: Generous: Do you think that being generous comes naturally to you, or is it something you actively have to work on?

Generosity is a two-way channel. It allows you to both give and receive. By sharing what you have, you create a positive flow of energy in your life.

If you feel you are not a two-way channel, write down an action you can take to be generous toward yourself. Remember, you first need to support your own system before offering it to others.

Question 3: Rejoice: Do you tend to feel jealous or envious of other people's financial success?

If you rejoice in others' success, you attract more of the same. Now, if you feel jealous or envious, don't criticize yourself. We are human beings. We have all kinds of emotions. Becoming aware of them is the first step in learning how to let them go. Think, with whom you can rejoice in their success? If it is too hard, start simple. Say "Good job!" to a stranger. Just make sure you start somewhere!

Question 4: Flexible: Are you physically flexible? Can you easily stretch yourself?

Being flexible opens you up to more opportunities.

If you are rigid, you send signals to the Universe that you are expecting money only through the source of your income. You are closing other channels that can bring money to you.

If you are rigid, it may reflect in your body, too. Do daily exercise to loosen your body's tightness.

Question 5: Action: Are you taking action to bring in money, or simply sitting on the couch and doing the affirmations?

Money loves action. The more action you take on your ideas, the more money you will attract.

As you step up to take one or all the above actions, see how many shifts you can make to cultivate your money mindset.

I hope this exercise has brought to your attention the simple actions you can take to elevate your vibrations and become a money-attracting factor in your life!

I would like to conclude by sharing my own mantra that keeps me moving forward:

1. Give yourself permission to be abundant!

2. Let not others define how you should be!

3. Always keep smiling to keep your vibrations high!

Apana Vemuri is an intuitive healer and spiritual mentor. From a young age, she had a spiritual bend of mind and channeled messages from other dimensions. With her patience and empathetic nature, her clients always feel welcomed and supported. Since 2010, Aparna has been helping people to break free from the cycle of physical, mental, emotional, and spiritual pain that has kept them stuck. She is passionate about creating a better world by bringing transformation at a personal level into every household. You can learn more about her here: https://www.aparnavemuri.com.

Get Aparna's free gift…

Abundance Unleashed: Reclaim Power over Mind,
a guided meditation, here:

https://OwnYourExpertiseBook.com/gifts

Chapter 14
Creating Harmony Through Consensus:
A Journey Toward a Better World
by Martie Weatherly

I think helping people live in peace is in my genes.

My maternal grandmother joined the Lifwynn Foundation—a group of psychoanalysts and patients who studied the inner struggle between harmony and conflict within a person's self as one navigates various situations and environments—in her twenties. She worked with them her entire life until her death at the age of 96. My aunt also worked and met her husband there, and my mother worked there occasionally, as well.

The foundation conducted groundbreaking research on how successful teams have a common set of values and beliefs, as well as a mutual understanding of each other's strengths and weaknesses.

The doctor who started Lifwynn owned a beautiful camp in the Adirondacks of upper New York. Every summer, my grandmother and I, along with the foundation's staff of eight and their family members, traveled there to live and work together. The atmosphere was one in which everyone, including children, was listened to with honor and respect. I was so lucky to experience such calmness and harmony, and I would try to emulate it later in my life.

I knew when I was 14 that I wanted to be a nurse. My dad wanted me to be a doctor, but I was set on the nursing profession. I realized later that I did not want the responsibility of people's life or death decisions. But I was attracted to the bedside care and connection with people.

At the age of 17, I went to Cornell University in Ithaca, NY, for two years and then to Cornell University-New York Hospital School of Nursing in the upper east side of New York for three years. I graduated with a bachelor's in nursing at the age of 22.

By then, I had met and married John, and was pregnant within two years. In those days, hospitals did not allow nurses to work once their pregnancy was showing, so I gave up my nursing job to be a mom.

Twelve years later, all my children were in school, which gave me a little extra time to go back to my profession. I took a refresher course and started working at the local hospital. This was the beginning of my nursing career for the next 48 years.

I was a very competent nurse, known for being a resource to everyone. However, I didn't think of myself as a leader and never put myself forward to take a more responsible position. Management seemed too difficult, as I would ask myself, "Who am I to tell them what to do? I don't want that burden."

When I was 44, John and I took the Landmark Forum, a course in personal development. That's how I learned that the stories I tell myself are not true—I made them up. This gave me more freedom to create new possibilities. John also learned some things about himself. He had been depressed for a few years and found that he really did not want to be married anymore. The fact that we could openly and calmly discuss something so tender was a breakthrough in our relationship.

Instead of being devastated, I was able to commit to a friendly, supportive, conflict-free relationship, and he felt the same. We celebrated all our children's weddings together with zero animosity. Many years later, I held his hand a few hours before his death.

I had also learned what it meant to stand for what I believe and move ahead to achieve that goal.

By the time I was 54, I began questioning which type of living arrangement would be best for me. I did not want to be in an apartment by myself, locking the door behind me and wishing I could visit my children.

Two years later, I was introduced to the idea of cohousing, a form of private home ownership in a community of members who share work and play and make decisions together based on consensus. This requires collaboration, listening to all points of view, before finding a creative solution that everyone is committed to following.

I found a group in Frederick, MD, the members of which were building a cohousing community of 38 homes. To me, the idea of consensus and coming to an agreement that everyone supports was the most important part of cohousing… not surprising for someone who grew up in an atmosphere of people calmly working things out together.

By making decisions by consensus, group members are able to find the best solution *for the whole group* at that time. Those solutions might not be exactly what I would want, but knowing they were best for the whole community was deeply satisfying.

In order for this to work, members must be able to put aside their personal preferences and find creative solutions everyone can buy into. There is no dissatisfied minority, and implementation is a done deal.

So, at the age of 58, I took a huge leap of faith and became a partner in developing Liberty Village. This meant that I was not only building a house, which I had never done, but also committing to a partnership to build the entire community. It required a huge amount of trust in myself, my partners, and our ability to work together and make things happen.

The day I moved into my house five years later was one of the most exciting days of my life!

One example of consensus in our community was when a new member wanted to move in and raise chickens. It took us several months to accept his chicken proposal. Once we had an agreement, though, we already had all the concerns handled, from how to prevent foxes from stealing the chickens to a way to be sure the rooster's crowing did not disturb the nearest neighbor. (The rooster was on probation for six months, and he passed.)

Because consensus fascinated me, I studied it more and more and eventually began teaching it to others. As a nurse, I had always been at the back of the room, following directions, supporting leaders, and being a resource for others. Now, people were coming to me for advice on a subject about which I was so passionate! I developed more confidence and enjoyed teaching it.

In my work with Landmark, I coached a group of six, which was the first time I had ever led a team. We produced amazing results together, and they gave me a ribbon that reads "#1 Coach," which I still have on my wall today. I was getting comfortable as a leader and a coach!

In the year 2000, I moved into my own home in my community, Liberty Village. The local hospital hired me as a supervisor, a leadership job I would never have imagined having years ago when I started my nursing career.

I was the highest administrative employee in the hospital, working mostly on my own, handling all the problems and staffing arrangements for the whole hospital overnight. I was amazed at my confidence and ability to manage.

My ability to communicate clearly and see another's point of view was a huge asset to that position, too. When a nurse complained to me that "The patient's family member is following me around asking when I am going to take him for a walk," I reminded her that the caregiver just needed reassurance that her relative was going to get his walk, and that the family member could actually be a resource to the nurse in regard to the best way to care for that particular patient.

Back at Liberty Village, we hired one of the best facilitation trainers to teach us facilitation. He wanted to create a two-year training for communities like ours. I latched onto that idea and suggested to my community that we be the first host community for his program. This meant enrolling everyone in providing lodging and food to about 20 people and devoting an entire weekend to tackling some of our weightiest problems. I was becoming more persuasive and enrolling!

That program is still going strong after 20 years! It is one of the things I have done in my life about which I am most proud. My existence was changing from follower to leader, creating new adventures!

I taught consensus to other communities and took a class from CoachU on coaching. I also pursued leadership training with Landmark Worldwide, which provided an enormous boost to my confidence, leadership, and outlook. As I became more confident in my coaching ability, I hired a coach and started coaching clients for a fee.

I loved the results my clients created as my business grew. For example, I supported a mother with her relationship with her teenage daughter, a business owner who found a way to get his four partners to talk to one another, another businessman who decided what career to follow, and a woman who cleaned the clutter out of her house. Varied situations, but all had a vision they were committed to yet unable to reach.

Then came COVID-19. Luckily, I had decided to leave my nursing job just before it hit, so I was spared the huge challenges that it put on healthcare workers. I hunkered down and worked from home from then on.

No retirement for me! I really wanted to be involved with people, supporting them in their commitment to make a difference in the world. I was looking to grow my little business to reach more people online and increase my income. I started taking courses with Alina Vincent to find my niche, which was initially business owners who felt stuck and wanted to move ahead.

I realized that my expertise and passion were in coaching communities whose consensus process was not working as well as they wanted. Doing so allowed me to nurture my commitment to people and teams working together in peace and harmony instead of struggle and upset. So, I implemented Alina's training to create a five-week online program to coach those communities. It was not easy to make that first program, as so much of it was brand new to me. I just kept saying, "I can do this" whenever I thought I could not.

To do this, I had to go way outside my comfort zone. I set up a "real" business, Weatherly Coaching, registered with the state, and hired a bookkeeper and a virtual assistant. I was registered to do business as Dreams to Action Coaching, which is exactly what I wanted (and still want) to bring to all my clients.

Doing that really warms my heart!

But most exciting was realizing that the ideas I had about improving the consensus process were spot on! When I heard the complaints people had about consensus, I developed my program to coach my participants with specific ideas they could take back to their communities. And it worked.

My participation in Alina's program was critical to my success in sharing the ideas of consensus. Step by step, she taught us how to create a five-week online course. I did exactly what she said. I transformed my bedroom into a recording studio and began to record zoom videos even if it took several do-overs.

I had learned a long time ago that I will get the most out of any coaching agreement if I show up, participate, and do the work, even when I catch myself resisting recommendations made. So, when Alina said to register people into my course first and then create the content, I did so. I enrolled people and created the content in good time.

Throughout this process, *I started to trust myself to make decisions on my own*. I decided when I should hire support staff, when I should have a course, and when I should hold off for a bit. Most importantly, I learned how to recover and move on when I experienced setbacks.

When my first program started, I led a discussion session every week. And every week, the same thought plagued me: *What am I going to say?* Of course, I (and my clients) always had plenty to say as we discussed the idea of consensus and how to use it in our communities.

I was thrilled by my participants' results, too.

One client lived in a community where one or two people consistently blocked proposals, causing all action around those proposals to cease. In my course, **Consensus: from Conflict to Creativity**, she found that communities could set aside a block if it was not in line with the community values. Now, her community has a way to keep going when a person blocks for an absolutely personal reason.

My graduates also found that they could impact the culture of their community in small ways that did not produce big waves or large pushback. Just by starting meetings with some method of bringing people together set the whole tone for the meeting and made reaching consensus easier.

Another simple tweak is to know when consensus should and should not be used. One community had one person who had not allowed the community to repair the common house for three years because they didn't like the color of paint selected. The color of paint is purely an opinion; this is not something that lends itself to creative decision-making. My participant was shocked that not all decisions had to be made with consensus. It gave her another way to approach the community about that issue.

As I continued to teach my courses, there was a point at which I said, "I really am an expert on consensus." The fact that it came as a surprise showed that I was moving past my blocks around not being as good as other consensus experts and owning my expertise.

I got great feedback from the participants, like:

"I learned so much."

"You gave me new ideas and different perspectives that we can try out in our situation."

"I have so much to bring back to my community."

With so many decisions to make, I also benefited greatly by having a supportive group of friends in Alina's mastermind right there cheering me on. When I was discouraged and heard, "Great idea, Martie! Your enthusiasm is wonderful," I could pick myself up and move on.

At one point, I was invited to speak to a group of business-people about consensus. Some of them use consensus in their teams and groups. Not surprisingly, they had the same challenges as the cohousing communities and were interested in bringing the ideas of consensus into their organizations and businesses.

I am delighted to be making so much difference to so many people! I am moving ahead in areas of my passion, finding more people outside of cohousing interested in collabora-tive decision-making.

I could not have imagined my life unfolding this way. *It was only because I discovered and owned my expertise that, at the age of 86, I am now enjoying a great business, surrounded by people who love my coaching.* I am taking on new challenges and opportunities as I share my ideas of working together in peace and harmony with more people than ever.

I encourage YOU to find the area of your expertise and share it with the world, too!

Here is my advice to anyone looking to get out of their own way in pursuit of a new undertaking:

1. **Get a good coach**, one who is right for you. And most importantly, take their advice, show up, participate, and implement!

2. **Put together a team of professionals to support you:** tax accountant, lawyer, bookkeeper, graphic designer, insurance agent, virtual assistant, and any others you need.

3. **Be open to learning and growing.** Most importantly, be coachable!

4. **Have a mentor**, someone who is an expert in your specific field, in whose footsteps you can follow.

5. **Find a community of support**—people who will listen when you need an ear and stand for you to succeed.

6. **Trust yourself** that you know your topic and have a lot of expertise to share.

7. **Fail forward.** Don't be afraid to fail, but always learn something from it.

Follow your passion to stay vibrant no matter how old you are!

Martie Weatherly is an empowerment coach who works with visionaries to transform the ideas in their heads into a thriving and productive business or organization, so they can make a real difference in the world. A life coach who has taught consensus for over twenty years, she helps her clients turn thoughts and dreams into actions and results. She is passionate about consensus decision-making, both in intentional communities and in any place where people want creative decisions that bring a solution with 100% buy-in. You can learn more about her here: https://coachmartie.coachesconsole.com.

Get Martie's free gift…

How to Build a Foundation for Successful Consensus Decision Making, a pdf to guide you in setting up a consensus meeting, here:

https://OwnYourExpertiseBook.com/gifts

ABOUT Alina Vincent

Alina Vincent is a business strategist, speaker, and international bestselling author of *Teach Your Expertise*, *Leverage Your Expertise* and *Monetize Your Expertise* books. She's known globally as the creator of the High Profit Programs blueprint and Profitable Online Challenges Formula, which helped her grow her business from zero to over a million dollars in just four years.

Alina is passionate about helping entrepreneurs package and monetize their knowledge and expertise to create a leveraged and scalable business. Experts hire her for strategic advice and a simple step-by-step approach to creating successful online programs, engaged Facebook communities, and profitable 5-day challenges.

Join her free Facebook community here: facebook.com/groups/BusinessOwnersWhoThinkBig.

BONUS GIFTS

This book comes with free gifts, exercises, and resources from each of the contributing authors.

You can access all of them on the bonus Resources Page:

OwnYourExpertiseBook.com/gifts

Made in the USA
Las Vegas, NV
29 August 2023

76768425R00115